The Avenue

A NEWCASTLE BACKSTREET BOYHOOD

SAMUEL W. HERBERT

The History Press

There are many to whom I would wish to dedicate this humble biography, but in my heart there is only one; a man none of you have ever met. He was kind and gentle, firm but fair; a reserved and quiet man, but a very brave one. A man who gave me a gentle smile only hours before the Lord took him away.

I am dedicating this book to my dear father.

First published 2012

The History Press
The Mill, Brimscombe Port
Stroud, Gloucestershire, GL5 2QG
www.thehistorypress.co.uk

British Library Cataloguing in Publication Data.
A catalogue record for this book is available from the British Library.

ISBN 978 0 7524 6886 0

Typesetting and origination by The History Press
Printed in Great Britain
Manufacturing managed by Jellyfish Print Solutions Ltd

Contents

Passing Thoughts

If the road you tread is stony
Long and often lonely
Should you think you are forsaken
Spurned and feel that fate has taken
All your hopes and dreams that mattered
Cast them down to lie there shattered
Should misfortune strike you often
Without the means the blows to soften
Lift your head and cry aloud
To him who dwells above the cloud
He will listen from up there
And give you courage your ills to bear.
As life's milestones pass you by
Lighten your step but do not sigh
Or think about the pain and sorrow
Of yesterday, there's still tomorrow
To come and go and thus unfold
The pleasures, joys and love untold
But when your journey's end is nigh
Count your blessings ere they fly
Then look back with gladness say
Thank you Lord for this sweet day.

Samuel W. Herbert

Acknowledgements

To my dear wife, who must have grown tired of gazing at the top of my head for three years as I scribbled for dear life.

To my children, who, by their keen interest in my activities as a youngster, inspired me to have a go at compiling this book.

To my daughter-in-law, who gave up a great deal of her leisure time to decipher my atrocious writing and put it into type.

To all my friends of bygone days.

Samuel W. Herbert

Introduction

Come on now, own up! How many of you thought I had lost my marbles when you first learned of my intention to embark upon what may, after all, prove to be an insuperable task? How many of you laughed at the idea of 'The Old Man' writing his autobiography? (Well, I had a damned good laugh myself – it seemed at first a ridiculous and over-ambitious venture!)

But why an autobiography? Why not a simple fictional story?

The answer, dear readers, is very simple; there is no need to resort to fiction to provide you with a story – my own life can assure an almost never-ending source of material. It can furnish stories which by no stretch of the imagination could I have manufactured.

That there will be problems I know and appreciate only too well, and the fact that I have never kept a diary will present especial difficulties, because not being able to refer back means I will have to rely solely on my memory. (How much easier it would have been to flick over the written pages of memory and find therein all the basic ingredients, and how convenient to find them in chronological order, thus needing only elaboration.) But there is no point in dwelling on what might have been, is there?

I was always an avid reader and I know that it is possible to become so absorbed in a story that one can imagine

oneself actually taking part in it. That's how I would like
you all to feel whilst you digest this humble effort.

I would like to say at once that whatever is lacking
in the sensational will be more than balanced by variety.
There are numerous amusing, even farcical episodes to
recount, but conversely there is much tragedy and sorrow.

It may surprise you to learn that my decision to
attempt a literary effort such as this could be the fulfil-
ment of a dream, one that was implanted in my mind
as I listened to the parting words of a man I hated and
despised: 'Providing you study hard on your way through
college, there is no reason why you should not do well
in the field of literature.' Thus spoke my Headmaster, Mr
Cook, a brilliant teacher but a tyrant of the old school!

I often wondered whether his prediction would have
borne fruit, and what his reaction would have been if his
number one target for the cane had proved him to be right!

You may well ask why I have waited until I was sev-
enty years old before tackling something which, after all,
may be beyond my ability to complete.

To be truthful, the circumstances of my life have
denied me the opportunity of making an earlier start; but
now, having enjoyed the exuberance of youth, accepted
and discharged the responsibilities of manhood and marriage, and savoured with some relief the less hectic years
of middle age, I am now, in the evening of my life, com-
pelled to live a much more peaceful one.

Surely then, with so much time on my hands, here is
the opportunity, now is the time to fulfil that dream.

I did say there would be problems and sure enough I
have found one I cannot overcome. 'Geordie' born and
bred though I am, I find it impossible to write in our
dialect, which is unique in expression but soul-shatter-
ing when attempting to portray in prose.

I have therefore decided that plain English will be the
only medium. So please remember when you are reading about the exploits of some raggy-arsed hooligans

(with affection!) that almost all of them spoke little else but down-to-earth 'Geordie' (yenaawarramean?)!

Now I have a decision to make – should I or should I not write my story in a clean and prissy manner? If I do, then all the stories concerning those aforementioned ruffians will sound empty and insipid. It would be impossible to describe adequately their antics and expressions in language and intonation more befitting public schoolboys.

On the other hand, if I get down to basics, then there has to be a frankness, which you may find distasteful. But I cannot forget the years I spent in a hell-hole with its accompaniment of brutality, obscenity and other soul-destroying indignities.

How then can I write a true story if I have to make liberal use of tinsel when relating certain incidents? I cannot compromise; therefore the realities of some situations in which I was involved – or witnessed – will be described in the actual language used at the time, which, dear readers, means an occasional use of four-letter words. My decision to be frank will be endorsed by the knowledge that you would prefer a true story rather than a fairytale.

Now that I am about to begin, I have opened one small door of my memory bank and there is, gushing forth, a veritable avalanche which almost overwhelms me, and such a gigantic hotchpotch of nostalgic incidents has to be thoroughly sorted out, which makes me appreciate to the full the magnitude of the task I have undertaken.

Finally, in order that continuity be preserved, I have taken advantage of many stories concerning my young life as told me by my brother Fred and sometimes by my parents.

So now, here it is, the story of my life as a boy and a young man.

I hope you enjoy it.

Samuel W. Herbert (1908-1983)
Newcastle, 1983

Chapter One

It was 1913 and spring was in the air, birds were twit-
tering, flowers were beginning to bloom and new-born
lambs were gambolling. 'Hey nonny nonny and tra-la-la!'

That's how it was on the day this chronicle begins;
but I certainly had no interest in those miracles of
nature, because I was perched precariously on top of the
garden railings that fronted my home. The trouble was
I couldn't move because one of those fiendishly sharp
spikes was firmly embedded in my bum! I had disobeyed
my parents' order not to climb and was now paying the
penalty. It felt like I had been there for ages. But crikey,
did I yell!

A passer-by came to the rescue and attempted to lift
me off, but unfortunately for me, the man didn't lift me
high enough and the damned spike ripped my back-side
open. The shriek I gave brought Mother racing out of
the house and she almost threw a fit when she saw the
blood pouring down my leg. There followed a frantic
dash to a doctor, who promptly ordered me to the Royal
Victoria Infirmary, where I had several stitches inserted
in my rear end.

Mother really went to town with me as we made our
way home. 'You are just an awkward young sod,' she
snapped, 'and don't think I am going to carry you all the
way home; you can walk, sore arse or no sore arse!'

That was bad enough, but after a few yards she stopped in her tracks. 'Oh my God, I've left your Dad's dinner in the oven,' she wailed. I maintained a discreet silence as she flew along Percy Street with me hoping, skipping and jumping behind her. She was muttering dire threats as we boarded a tram. 'If that dinner is ruined you *will* have a sore arse!'

I wish I could have written that there was a happy ending to that gallop back home, but it was not to be. Mother dashed into the scullery, flung open the oven door and made a hasty grab at the dish inside. I swear that flames were coming down her nostrils when she withdrew the pathetic remains of Dad's favourite meal. 'Look at that,' she said with a sob. 'Burnt to a bloody cinder!'

Of course, Dad *would* have to enter the scullery at that moment to see Mother standing there with the blackened remains of a bunny in her hands. He gave it a curious look. 'What the hell's that?' he asked. 'It's your dinner – rabbit pie,' she moaned. 'Funny bloody rabbit pie that is!' he snorted. He removed his jacket and then said, 'How did you come to burn it, been gossiping have you?'

Mother's face went all colours and for a moment I thought she was about to christen me with the smouldering pie.

'No, I haven't been gossiping! I have been to the Infirmary to have your son's arse stitched!'

All that happened sixty-seven years ago, on a spot not fifty yards from where I live now.

Shortly after I returned to this area I watched, with not a little sadness, the demolition of the house where I spent my early childhood, to make way for a new housing estate.

As I watched, I remembered my brother, Fred, racing along the street in his knickerbockers (which he hated) and my first boyhood friend – Geordie Royle – sporting the finest brace of green candles on his upper lip one would never wish to see! Looking through my window today I can see many familiar landmarks from the old days, the most important being St James's Church, my first Sunday school.

At the time this story begins, I was living with my parents and brother Fred in Gill Street, Benwell, a working class suburb of Newcastle. Fred was then seven years old and I was almost five, and Dad was a miner employed at a local colliery.

I suppose everyone has come to accept miners as rough, tough and not impartial to a belly of beer, but nothing could be further from the truth as far as Dad was concerned. He was quiet and reserved, indeed almost an introvert, but he lived only for his home and family.

Yet there was something about him, something indefinable that suggested he was not of true mining stock; he was also very intelligent, well read and spoke clear English without any trace of the Northumbrian 'burr'. Fred and I were not allowed to use the Geordie dialect – at least not in his presence. He had a fetish for personal cleanliness and he was always meticulously dressed. His pride and joy was his moustache, which he groomed almost reverently. It would have been difficult to visualise any man looking less like a miner than he. We two kids adored him.

Mother was a very handsome woman and with her copper coloured hair and fashionably slim waist she made the perfect partner for Dad.

Brother Fred? Well, he was a sturdy lad with an infectious grin; he was also stubbornly independent. He did very well at the local school. He had one pet anathema – his knickerbockers. In those days they were not uncommon, but they were worn mostly by boys whose fathers were a little higher in the social scale than ours! Certainly in our part of the world, miners' sons did not wear trousers that were fastened under the knee by a piece of fancy ribbon! Poor Fred had to endure a lot of leg-pulling before he was allowed to discard what had become known as his 'cacky catchers'– much to his relief.

Trying to describe myself isn't easy, but of one thing I am sure; I was very often the despair of my parents. I didn't have to look for trouble, it was usually just around the corner, and if there was a hole anywhere, I would fall into it. In fact my father often shook his head in wonderment at my unhappy propensity for incurring cuts and bruises.

Poor dear Dad, he was never to hear the half of it, but between the four of us there was a bond of affection that was never to wane.

In those far off, peaceful days in Benwell, very little out of the ordinary ever happened (unless you count the punctured backside incident) but there was one aspect of our lives we two lads found puzzling.

At the time we lived in Gill Street. Father's family lived in Condercum Road, not more than a hundred yards away, but never once did he visit them, nor they us. Fred and I knew where they lived – we had often seen them standing at their front door – but we had never spoken to them because we had been given explicit orders not to. Of course we wondered why.

There was also some sort of mystery about my Mother's family; her father visited us regularly, but neither Fred nor I had ever seen our maternal grandmother. There wasn't even a photograph of her, which was most odd in those days when every household had a family album. So where was she? What did she look like? Whenever we asked those questions, we were told to 'shut up' and even Mother, throughout her long life, never talked about her. Obviously there must have been very strong reasons for the extraordinary secrecy concerning her and it never seemed worth the effort to try and solve the mystery.

However, my father's photograph albums provided a wealth of information about his side of the family; when Fred and I were old enough to understand, Dad used them to explain his ancestry – way back into the eighteenth century. Sadly though, those albums mysteriously disappeared.

Chapter Two

In 1868 a certain Mr Herbert died at the cruelly early age of thirty-three, leaving a widow and two sons aged four and two. He had been a college lecturer, and by all accounts he had a great future before him. He had been a fairly wealthy man and left his family well provided for. The elder son followed in his father's footsteps and became a lecturer and the younger went to live with relatives in Australia.

In 1887 the elder son, who was then twenty-seven years old, married a girl named Martha Simpson. He went against the wishes of his mother, who showed her displeasure by changing her will and leaving everything to the younger son.

Tragedy struck again in 1900 when the eldest son died aged just forty, leaving a widow, three sons and a daughter. The names of the four children were Samuel (the oldest), James, John and Martha. Unfortunately, he left them, if not exactly in poverty, with little money to throw about.

Trying to rear four children on such limited resources proved too much for Martha. After only a few months she found herself in difficulties and asked her mother-in-law for some assistance. The mother-in-law refused. Then Martha suddenly declared her intention to re-marry.

Samuel was then thirteen years old and he reacted violently against the proposed marriage. He had apparently met his future stepfather and the feeling for each other had been mutual – instant dislike! Despite his strong protests his mother married the man – a cobbler by the name of Joseph Lambert.

Sam's dislike of his stepfather continued to fester, then it erupted into open hostility. It hadn't made him feel any less resentful when he realised that his brothers and sister had accepted the 'usurper' without demur, so he made his feelings known in no uncertain manner.

Because of his antagonism towards his stepfather, coupled with the strained relations between him and the rest of the family, it became obvious that drastic measures would have to be taken. Family relations became increasingly strained.

It was Sam himself who solved the problem. Greatly daring, he visited his father's mother – she who had refused financial help – and poured out his troubles. To his surprise (and delight) she not only listened to him but asked him to go and live with her.

Everything went smoothly for him during the following year, but on the one occasion when he visited his family, he realised that no one was very much interested in him. In fact, the reception they gave him was so cool he decided there was no point in going back. Four years were to elapse before he stood in their house again.

Shortly before his fourteenth birthday, his grandmother staggered him with the news that she had made arrangements for him to attend a grammar school; no doubt she had visions of him following in the footsteps of his father and grandfather. Sam, however, had other ideas and gently but firmly told her he had no wish to attend another school.

Naturally she was very angry, but she was horrified when he told her that when he was fourteen years old he was going to be a miner!

Why would an intelligent young man decide to follow an occupation that was not only dirty and dangerous, but at that time decidedly non-lucrative? When his grand-mother asked him the reason for such an outrageous decision, he replied, 'Ever since I can remember, school books have dominated my life, and I want no more of them.'

But was that really true? There was no doubt that he had a chip on his shoulder as big as an oak tree because of the loss of his father and the advent of a stepfather, but it doesn't explain his decision.

Whatever the reason, he refused to reconsider what his grandmother referred to as 'the decision of an ungrateful young idiot'. She gave him an ultimatum – either go to grammar school or return home to his mother.

He had no intention of doing either, and his grand-mother, sensing his determination, relented slightly and allowed him to stay with her until she asked a distant aunt of his to give him lodging.

One week after his fourteenth birthday Sam began his career as a miner in a local colliery, and he continued living with his aunt for the next four years.

He originally intended to start with a trial period of about six months, but before the time was up he con-fessed to his aunt that he was having doubts; the working conditions below ground were appalling and the fatality rate was distressingly high. Nevertheless, at the end of six months he decided to make mining his permanent career.

He was aware that more efficient methods of coal production were to be introduced, that new coalfields were being explored and new shafts were to be sunk. He therefore reasoned that there would be plenty of opportunities to make the grade in the managerial side of mining – if he was prepared to study.

So with some considerable practical help from his aunt – to whom he had become very attached – he worked hard and studied diligently. After three years it became apparent to his bosses that he was destined to reach the top.

Meanwhile, his family had moved into a house in Condercum Road, Benwell, and he discovered that he now had a half-brother and sister. He was highly amused when he learned how appalled they had been at his decision to be a mine-worker. He simply dismissed them as 'pompous sods'!

Shortly after his seventeenth birthday, Samuel met and began to court a girl called Ethel Henderson. She was not greatly enamoured of his occupation and tried many times to persuade him to give it up. (Her father was not too happy at the prospect of having a miner as a son-in-law either.) But Sam was adamant – mining was his career.

Their courtship continued strongly but too ardently, because in the autumn of 1905 Ethel told him she was pregnant.

He sought the advice of his aunt. 'You will have to visit your parents, and explain everything to them,' she told him.

He hadn't visited his family for almost four years, so it is easy to imagine their astonishment when he calmly walked in on them. They were shattered when he told them that he was going to have to get married, and piously condemned his 'lecherous conduct'. Because he was still a minor, their written consent to the marriage was necessary by law – and they spitefully refused to give it.

However, his aunt interceded on his behalf and some very strong words from her made them change their minds.

So, in July 1906, Mr and Mrs S.W. Herbert became the parents of a son, who was duly named John Frederick George – the names of his grandfather and great-grandfather.

Another son followed in September of 1908; he was named after his father, Samuel William. You've probably guessed who those two boys were – my brother Fred and myself.

Chapter Three

As the summer of 1913 drifted by it seemed that Fred and I had all the time in the world to indulge in boyhood pleasures. One very enjoyable feature of our lives was the regular Sunday outing to the beautiful Tyne Valley. Dad would hire a pony trap and it was a joy to be hauled along by a trotting pony while breathing in God's fresh air.

Dad had been a miner for almost eleven years and he was beginning to reap the fruits of his hard work and study. Besides holding a deputy-overman certificate, he was also an explosives expert. Sadly there was many a bitter quarrel between him and Mother. Despite his good progress and the years he had spent working towards such a high position, she was still trying to persuade him to give it up. I suppose it was her concern for his safety underground that drove her to make so many ineffectual attempts to get him to pack it in. She somehow lacked the philosophical stoicism possessed by many miners and their wives.

The strained atmosphere after these quarrels usually lasted for a few days, so we two kids were not unduly perturbed when, following one particular row shortly after my fifth birthday, there was the usual unpleasant silence. We soon realised that the latest row was much more intense than any of the others we had witnessed, because, even though the air cleared as it normally did,

Dad began to display a brusqueness that was not only alien to his nature but most disconcerting to we two lads.

As the days passed without any appreciable difference in his manner, we began to wonder whether he was ill, or maybe extremely worried. But our questions to Mother simply evoked such answers as 'No, he is not ill' or 'Don't bother your father just now.' Certainly it was all very mysterious.

Weeks passed before his natural good nature reasserted itself (much to our relief) but within a few days there began a sequence of events that was to culminate in a complete upheaval in our lives.

It all began one day early in November. Due to some reorganisation at the colliery, Dad had been asked to work a twelve-hour shift beginning at 4 a.m., which meant he would arrive back home about 4 p.m.

I had been attending school for six weeks and on the day in question, Fred and I were preparing to return to school after the dinner break. As we approached the yard door we were shocked to see it flung open violently. Dad entered in a raging temper. He savagely flung his bike into the shed and stormed into the scullery. 'Get my bath ready,' he snarled at our astonished Mother. I don't think he noticed us!

'Off to school you two,' snapped Mother, and mystified though we were, we knew better than to ask questions. When we returned from school, Dad was not at home and Mother was looking extremely upset – but she remained tight-lipped.

Just after tea there was a knock on the door. Mother opened it and in came the vicar of our church. A short time later Dad returned and he immediately retired to the front room, accompanied by the vicar. A visit from the vicar was unusual to say the least, but when he and Dad were in deep conversation for almost two hours it meant only one thing – trouble! That was confirmed later when Mother joined them in the front room and returned crying.

More surprises were in store for us the following morning. Dad was sitting in the kitchen and told us in a quiet voice that he would not be returning to the colliery. He also said quite firmly that there were to be no more questions from us.

Enlightenment began to dawn on us when we reached school. After the usual prayers in the Assembly Hall, the Head asked us all to say a prayer for two of our fellow pupils, whose father had been killed in an accident in the colliery where Dad worked. Of course we then realised why he had returned home early on the day of the accident, but what still puzzled us was why had he been so badly affected? There had been other fatal accidents in that colliery but the effect on Dad's mood had just been temporary.

We mentioned the prayer to him when we were having dinner and he told us that the dead man had been one of his colleagues, but he gave no explanation for his decision not to return to the colliery.

During the following week our home was a hive of activity. Dad had left on the Monday for regions unknown to Fred and I – although Mother knew where he was – and Granddad Henderson visited us almost every evening. It was obvious, even to us, that something was about to happen; there could be no other reason for Mother's constant tears.

The climax came on Thursday as we were preparing for bed. Dad handed Fred a letter and said, 'Give this to the Headmaster tomorrow morning.'

'What is it?' asked a naturally puzzled Fred.

Dad paused for a while before answering. 'You will not be returning to that school after tomorrow.' We both gaped at him, then he added, 'We are moving away from here some time next week. I am going to work in another colliery in Ashington.' He surely must have realised that there were many questions we wanted to ask because in a very grave tone of voice he said, 'Some day, when you are both old enough to understand, I will explain to you the reason for this sudden move.'

And with that we had to be content.

'Fred, where is Ashington?' I asked.

'Hundreds of miles over there!' he replied, pointing a finger in a vague direction.

'Oh.'

'Like Alice said, it gets curioser and curioser,' quoted my brother.

'Who is she?'

'Who is who?'

'Alice?'

He replied with a withering look, 'Goodbye Benwell!'

Chapter Four

The four of us stood in the kitchen of our new home. Dad was anxiously awaiting Mother's reaction to the strange surroundings.

'Nice and clean,' she said at last, but with a marked lack of enthusiasm.

Two weeks had passed since Dad informed us we were leaving Benwell – two very hectic weeks. He had spent the first week at Ashington finalising the essential details of work and accommodation. On the Thursday of the second week we bade goodbye to Benwell and all our friends.

Our new home, in common with most colliery houses, was small. What surprised Fred and me was that it had been re-painted, scrubbed out and the larder stocked with food. We kids were, of course, unaware that Mother had two married aunts living in Ashington, who had rallied round to help.

Both their husbands were employed at Ashington Colliery. We owed a debt of gratitude to those two ladies and Mother was quick to say so. She had been painfully quiet during the previous fortnight but she brightened up very soon. However, her brightness was shattered after we had our meal.

She went into the yard, presumably on a tour of inspection, and after a few minutes we heard a 'whoop' followed by a strangled snort.

With some alarm we watched as she tottered into the kitchen; she had her nose pinched with one hand and the other hand was tremulously pointing in the direction of the yard.

'What's that out there?' she squeaked.

'What's what?' asked Dad

'That flaming netty!' she yelled.

'What's wrong with it?' he asked, hiding a smile.

'What's wrong with it?' she shouted, 'It's a dry netty, that's what's wrong with it. And it's putrid,' she continued, 'and if you think I am going to use it then you can think again!' (Off we go again, I thought.)

There followed a right old barney between them, but she refused to be placated, would not accept any compromise – she wanted a 'wet netty' or nothing (she even hinted that she would return to Newcastle). Finally, when his patience was almost at breaking point, Dad enlisted the help of her aunts, who talked to her long and earnestly. Eventually, having been assured that plans were well advanced for the installation of 'wet netties', she accepted the position, much to everyone's relief.

It can't be denied that those dry closets were an abomination, and when the day came for them to be emptied (by men with no sense of smell and equipped with cast-iron stomachs) the stench was appalling and permeated the atmosphere for miles around.

You know something? We never did see those flush toilets!

Moving to a strange town can bring an abundance of difficulties. If, as often happens in small communities, the locals are closely knit, there can be open resentment of outsiders. At that time Ashington was little more than a village, but those marvellous people accepted us almost immediately, and we found that settling down was comparatively easy.

Having been unemployed for a few weeks, Dad was short of money, and Christmas would have been a really

dull affair had it not been for the generosity of my
Mother's aunts.

After a couple of months however, there was not only
a marked improvement in our finances, but Mother had
become a little more cheerful. That was due mainly to
her acceptance of the inevitable – Dad's determination
to pursue his mining career.

He looked more content, and the worried, haunted
look that had appeared on his face before leaving Benwell
had been completely wiped away. I was also very sure that
he had derived great satisfaction from the knowledge that
he'd been right in deciding to leave Benwell.

Our home was beginning to look brighter and much
more comfortable due to the addition of new furniture. All
in all, life was pleasant and the future looked very promising.

Fred, however, wasn't at all happy in our new surroundings. He had become extremely reticent and
seldom ventured out of doors. We were all aware of his
resentment at having to leave Benwell, but two months
should have been ample time to get over it. His problem
was brought to light one evening when Dad chided him
for his surliness. When Dad asked a question he always
demanded a verbal reply – 'Shoulder shrugging is for
mutes,' he would say.

He looked on in amazement as Fred began to explain
(or tried to). He was stammering something terrible.
Whatever the cause, and Fred was as mystified as anyone,
that damned affliction was to remain with him all his life.

Chapter Five

A little over three months had elapsed since we arrived in Ashington, and the transformation in our family life was truly remarkable. Dad had settled down and was doing exceedingly well at the colliery. There was little doubt that he was destined for a high position.

We kids were quite happy, and though Fred occasionally hankered for Gill Street and his former friends, we had settled in well at our new school. Life indeed was carefree during the spring of that year.

June brought with it some lovely weather and as we were then enjoying our summer holidays from school, Dad used whatever spare time he had to take all of us to the neighbouring countryside, or on special occasions, to the coast.

One Sunday in that particular month was most surprising. When we left for an outing with Dad, Mother didn't come with us. Both of Mother's aunts were at our house. When I asked Dad why Mother wasn't coming, he muttered something about a stork.

I was only five and a half years old, so I thought perhaps a stork was some kind of chicken. It was only when we arrived back that comprehension dawned – a new baby had arrived. She was called Ethel.

In July, a cloud of depression appeared to affect the whole of the community. It was normal practice for neighbours to congregate around the back doors and indulge in light-hearted gossip, but towards the end of that month their faces were grave and the over-riding topic of conversation was some stinker by the name of Kaiser.

'Fred,' I asked, 'who is this fellow Kaiser?'

'Who?'

'Kaiser.'

'You mean Kyser, stupid.'

'Well, who is he?'

'Oh, you're too young to understand,' (Fred was a very old eight-year-old!).

And there the matter ended, because Dad wouldn't enlighten me either.

However, towards the end of that month Dad at last answered my persistent questions. I learned that the geezer called Kyser was some kind of king who was going to have his arse kicked. Nevertheless, whoever he was, he was the cause of the first barney my parents had had for months.

Near the end of that month, Dad had attended a meeting at the local Miners' Hall, and when he returned home Ma looked at him carefully, then she bawled, 'Well, what happened?' Dad divested himself of his jacket before answering. 'There is some talk of forming a new battalion of the Northumberland Fusiliers, and if men should ever be needed then most of us will join.'

Mother pursed her lips. 'There is no need for any of you to volunteer just yet,' she snapped.

But Dad was in no mood for arguments. 'Thousands of men have already lost their lives, and if the call should come for volunteers then I shall go.' And with that Mother had to be content.

Whatever it was that had cast a dark shadow and gravened the faces of those normally ebullient people was much too complicated for me to understand. However, I soon began to realise what it was all about during the weeks that followed. Almost every day there were tearful goodbyes as, one after another, the able-bodied men offered their services to king and country.

Boys my age (who could chew tobacco and expel the juices with as much dexterity as their fathers) would proudly announce that theirs fathers or brothers had joined the forces. Even then I was much too young to understand the magnitude of what was happening, or that the slaughter which was to affect the lives of millions had begun.

Our family life continued much as normal, although, as in other households, there was obvious tension and gravity, with Mother quiet and apprehensive and Dad equally quiet, but thoughtful.

August and September passed before the full impact of the situation hit us with brutal clarity. Just two weeks after my sixth birthday, Dad, who had been on the early shift, didn't arrive home until late in the afternoon. Mother was about to ask him where he had been when he said, very quietly, 'I have joined the Northumberland Fusiliers.'

I won't dwell on the tearful scene that followed; no doubt the thought uppermost in Mother's mind would be similar to those of other wives and mothers whose menfolk had gone: 'What's going to happen to us all?' But all credit to Dad for doing what untold numbers of other men had done.

So, one day in October 1914, I watched Dad walk through the front door, on his way, with head held high, to fight the Germans.

It was a hateful month and neither Fred nor I could really believe that Dad had gone, but Mother had recovered from the shock of his departure enough to display a degree of cheerfulness.

As the days passed we resumed an almost normal life. After all, most of our friends had been deprived of their menfolk, and like them we had to be cheerful and optimistic about the future. A couple of letters from Dad helped to ease the strain.

November was uneventful, but December saw the beginning of a radical change in Mother's behaviour. She became irritable and bad tempered, as I found to my cost when I came home one evening with the arse of my trousers missing. She gave me a whale of a hiding, and in the process of having my arse tanned I gained a new insight into the character of Fred.

'Leave him alone,' he shouted. 'You wouldn't have done that if Dad had been here!'

Stunned at such rebellion she gaped at him, then, very surprisingly, she quietly ordered us both to bed.

Never before had either of us been the victims of such violent punishment from our parents. Mother was usually reasonably tolerant to misbehaviour, so her lapse was difficult to understand. Actually, we two kids were too young to realise that it was her constant anxiety regarding Dad, plus the fact that Christmas was almost upon us, which caused her frequent bouts of ill-temper.

During that difficult period we had good reason to be eternally grateful to Mother's two aunts, not only for their practical help, but also for their cheerfulness and optimism, which helped enormously in lifting Mother out of the well of depression into which she was sinking. But bad things happen to good people and there was tragedy on the horizon for one of those dear ladies. She received the dreaded communication from the War Office informing her that her son had been killed in action. With cruel irony it arrived on the same day that Mother had a letter from Dad telling her he was coming home on leave.

It reminded Mother that she was only one of countless numbers of mothers and wives who had loved ones in the forces, and who had to bear the uncertainty with courage.

We looked forward with great pleasure to Dad's arrival, and when the day came Fred and I were out early – he at one end of the street and I at the other.

The seven days he spent with us passed all too quickly. During that week yet another momentous decision was made and, once again, our lives were to be profoundly affected.

Chapter Six

Midway through Dad's leave, Mother dropped a bomb-shell. 'I am thinking of going back to Newcastle until the war is over.'

Dad looked dumbfounded but said nothing as she added, 'I cannot live here any longer on my own. If I return to Newcastle I will at least have Bella (her sister) and Father for company.'

For a while Dad sat and looked at her as though lost for words – most probably it had never occurred to him that such an eventuality would ever arise – but when he did answer her it was obvious that he was very angry. Hadn't he worked hard to get a nice house put together? Weren't the kids happy living here? Wasn't she among good neighbours and didn't she have two kind-hearted aunts living beside her?

Whatever Dad said, Mother was not to be diverted from her decision to return to the city. I have no doubt that it was his reluctance to have his leave marred by prolonged argument which made him say that she must do what she thought was best for us.

The argument broke anew when Granddad arrived the following day. In no uncertain terms he lambasted Mother for her stupidity. He warned her that there were no decent houses available in the city, and he also pointed out that he and her uncles had used their influence to get them to Ashington in the first place. But his forceful arguments didn't make the slightest impression on her – her mind was made up.

I think her decision to leave Ashington had the worst effect on her aunts. They protested and begged her to give the matter a little more thought, but Mother remained obdurate, so the bitterly disappointed aunts retired from the fray.

Fred and I were shattered by the news of another move. In fact it was surprising how bitter Fred was because he, more than anyone, had resented moving to Ashington in the first place. But he had come to like Ashington and he didn't hesitate to say so. However, the decision had been made, and after little more than a year in those pleasant surroundings we were to be uprooted once again. Our new address? 'Wait and see,' replied Mother.

Two months later, Mother received a letter from Dad containing the unhappy news that he had left his previous location but could not give any further information regarding his destination. Any future letters from her would have to be addressed to an army post office. This could mean only one thing – that he had gone, or was preparing to go into an area of hostilities – and Mother became very upset. Those two good aunts comforted her as best they could and had another go at persuading her to remain in Ashington, but if anything she was more determined than ever to leave.

We boys had been transferred to another school and had become extremely unsettled.

As the days passed, Mother became more and more irritable, and though she had made frequent visits to Newcastle she refused to say when or if we would be moving. We could only hope she would have a change of heart. It was not to be.

The countdown to the move began on a Saturday morning, when she received a letter. She didn't say who it was from, but after reading it she savagely tore it into little pieces.

'I have to go to Newcastle,' she said a little later, but to our surprise she told us that we were to remain behind in the care of one of her aunts.

Whatever the reason for the visit, it proved to be a very lengthy one, because she didn't arrive back home until after tea – and she appeared to be in a towering rage. That didn't deter Fred from asking her once again whether or not we were moving. 'We are moving next week,' she snapped.

We had more fun and games when Granddad arrived on the Sunday afternoon, no doubt hoping that Mother had changed her mind. When she told him she hadn't and announced the address of our new house he almost screamed with rage.

'Have you taken leave of your senses?' he roared. She didn't reply. Then he continued, 'Surely you are not going to live in that bloody hole?' She refused to discuss the matter so Granddad, red-faced with anger and exasperation, made an abrupt departure.

This was a most distressing period for Fred and me, and Granddad's remark about a 'bloody hole' didn't make us feel much better. Neither did the fact that Mother had decided to dispose of some of the larger items of furniture.

'There won't be enough room for it all,' she told Granddad. He was a little startled, 'No room, how big is the flaming place?' he asked. 'It will be big enough for us,' she replied.

He shook his head in dismay, but despite everything, he promised to come by the following weekend and help us with the packing.

During the last few days before our departure, Fred and I talked many times about our future. He was almost nine years old by then and very intelligent. He was convinced that Mother was making a very bad mistake by moving, and he was firmly of the opinion that Dad had not left Gill Street merely to work in another colliery. 'Something bad happened,' he would say with conviction.

The bane of his life though was his stammer. He spent hours reading aloud and even resorted to singing – during which, oddly enough, he never stammered – but it all proved futile.

When we retired to our beds for the last time in Ashington we lay for some time talking about various things, then he quite suddenly said, 'Mother has been anxious to move, so now that we are, why is she looking so worried?'

I neither knew nor cared.

Goodbye, Ashington!

Chapter Seven

We were all very, very tired on that late Monday afternoon in March 1915. I am sure that Mother, Granddad,
baby Ethel, Fred and I looked a pathetic quintet as we
passed through the monstrous portico of the Central
Station.

We had been going at it since the crack of dawn,
packing the remainder of our goods. Those had been
despatched by carrier and we followed on later.

Mother's aunts, who had been so kind to us, had not
hesitated to voice their disapproval of the move, but had
called to say goodbye. Their concern for us was touching
but many years were to pass before we were to see those
good people again.

As if it was not depressing enough, it had started to
rain, and, as I looked idly around, I got the impression
that those high, dark buildings were gazing at us with
malevolence, sneering, 'Welcome back.'

Truly they were the personification of this dreary,
dirty city. Fred had been extremely quiet almost all that
day – a fact that Mother commented on as we waited for
a tram. 'When are you going to straighten your face?' she
asked him. He just shrugged his shoulders, but that shrug
spoke volumes.

Granddad was also becoming a little grumpy. We discovered just how irritable he was when a tram arrived.

'Hurry up Ethel, I'm bloody soaked,' he bawled at Mother.

'Hurry up, for Christ's sake,' he roared at Fred.

'Get a bloody move on,' he snarled at me.

The unsuspecting conductor looked at the ten shilling note Granddad gave him for the fares. 'Have you nothing smaller?' he asked. Following Granddad's reply I am sure that many conductors would have thrown us off the tram.

Mother had said our new home wasn't far from the station and I gazed out the window expectantly.

The tram clanked its way up a fairly steep hill, turned left when it reached the top and after a short distance came to a stop outside a church. (I wasn't to know it, but that church was to have a great influence on me during the years that followed).

We alighted and, with Granddad carrying baby Ethel, we walked about fifty yards. We reached what appeared to be a back lane. 'Right,' said Mother, 'this is it.' She turned into the lane and as I followed her I glanced up to read the nameplate. It read 'The Avenue'.

I now know that there should have been another plate baring the words 'Abandon hope all ye who enter here'.

It was almost dark, which did little to enhance the appearance of what could only be described as a dirty back lane. In those days of course, streets were lit solely by feeble gas lamps, which cast sinister shadows.

We toddled along behind Mother, listening to Granddad airing his feelings in no uncertain manner. 'It bloody stinks, what the hell were you thinking about?'

It was beginning to rain heavily and the baby had cried almost continuously since leaving Ashington. Not surprisingly, Mother's temper had become a little frayed and she snapped at Granddad. Fred was still singularly silent and I felt worried and confused.

No doubt because of the rain, very few people were on the street, but we did see plenty of nosy-parkers peeping through their windows at the new arrivals.

As far as I could see, the houses were built on one side of the lane, with the other side flanked by what appeared to be large garage doors. We passed one block of straggling houses and came to another narrow lane that bisected The Avenue. I could see some small shops, whose windows cast ghostly reflections from their flickering gas lamps.

We were mid-way through the next block of dingy looking houses when Mother said, 'Here we are then.' She was pointing to a flight of stone steps leading from the pavement to a large front door.

We followed as she climbed the steps and pushed the door open. Behind it was a small passage with another door to the right of it, and on the left we could see a staircase leading to the upper regions. Granddad took the key from Mother and unlocked the door to the right and stepped inside what was to be our future home. He fished around his pockets and eventually found a box of matches, with which he lit the gaslight. There, in all its glory, was our new residence – welcome to 88 The Avenue!

Fred and I were now not only wet, cold, hungry and tired – we were speechless with disbelief when we entered that musty smelling room. Granddad was the first to react.

'Have you taken leave of your senses, woman?' he asked Mother. She didn't answer and he shook his head as if in disgust, then said, 'Well, I'm off, better get your bloody sister to help you.' He turned and left without another word.

It was unbelievable. This single room with filthy wallpaper hanging from the walls, a rusty fireplace, a filthy, grease-smeared sink, a bare floor with only the ragged remains of a clippy mat covering it, this was to be our home?

For furniture there was an old couch, our own table and four chairs, our own dressing table and what appeared to be a wardrobe, but where was the rest of our furniture? Where was our room, and more to the point, where were our beds?

'We'll be living here for just a short time, I shall get a better place soon,' said Mother, answering our unspoken questions.

She began attending to the baby and Fred and I sat on the rickety couch, sick and thoroughly fed-up.

Having changed and fed the baby, Mother opened what appeared to be a cupboard door. 'Your two beds are in there,' she said, pointing inside. 'Inside there?' asked Fred. 'Yes,' she answered. Fred poked his head inside then hurriedly stepped back. 'I am not sleeping in there,' he said with emphasis. Mother lit a candle and went inside what was commonly called a box-room, but this one had been used for very small boxes! Actually, it resembled one of those cupboards that are usually found under staircases. The ceiling was the underside of the stairs leading from the passage and the floor was L-shaped.

There was one bed on the base of the L with the other on the upright and there was only a six-inch gap between them.

Once again Fred expressed his displeasure, 'I'm not going to sleep in there,' he said angrily. I can still picture him, tight-lipped and mutinous as he stood glaring at Mother.

'You'll have to put up with it for a short while, at least until I can get a better place,' she said. The outcome, of course, was inevitable – we had to sleep in the black hole.

Nature can call upon one at the most awkward of times – as it did shortly after we had inspected our room.

'Mother, where's the netty?' I asked.

'Why?'

'I want to go.'

She walked to the sink and brought forth a bucket that was standing under it. 'Use that,' she said. I looked at the bucket, then at Fred, who yelled, 'There is a toilet, isn't there?' Mother sighed then picked up a key lying on the dirty mantelpiece. 'Come on then,' she snapped.

I followed her through the front door and down the stone steps leading to the pavement. She then did a U-turn and descended another short flight of steps leading to a kind of passage, on a level with the basements. The other end of the tunnel opened on to some kind of courtyard, dimly illuminated by the eerie glow of a dyspeptic gas lamp. There were two houses in that evil-smelling area, and on each side were a number of what looked like small sheds – obviously the netties. Mother opened the door of one of them and the nauseating stench that emanated from the inside made me want to vomit. How ironic that even in primitive Ashington the toilet – albeit a dry one – was sited in our own backyard.

Mother left me on my own and I didn't waste time before galloping back to discover that we had some visitors – Mother's sister Bella (who I was seeing for the first time) and five of her daughters.

It was an amusing encounter really; Fred was sitting on the settee, looking at his scruffy cousins in a lofty and disdainful manner, while they were poking their tongues out at him. When I entered, they concentrated on me, but I, unlike Fred, retaliated by poking out my tongue back at them. And in doing so I planted in Bella a feeling of dislike for me which was immediately apparent when she snarled, 'Don't poke your tongue out you cheeky young sod!'

Mother took us both to task for not greeting our cousins in a more cordial manner, but Fred, obviously thinking of something else, suddenly asked, 'Does Dad know we have moved into this place?' Mother glared at him but didn't answer.

By the time we had unpacked the remainder of our belongings, it was almost time for our beds, but Fred decided that he too would have to pay a visit to the netty, so I escorted him to the yard. His disgust knew no bounds, especially when a bloody great rat bounded out of the netty when he opened the door. With a yell he leaped back and then he slammed the door shut and pissed on the outside of it!

He was absolutely furious and for the first time ever I thought Mother was going to strike him when he asked, 'Why have you brought us to this stinking place?' She pooh-poohed the idea that we had seen a rat but he continued to argue. She lifted her hand to him but he, red-faced and defiant, didn't back away. She sighed and dropped her hand. 'Go to bed,' she said, wearily.

Our room was illuminated by two candles in holders, nailed to the wall. In all fairness our beds and bedding looked spotlessly clean.

As I was undressing, I had a sudden thought. I looked out and said, 'Mother, where is your bed?' She pointed to the wardrobe. When she opened the doors I saw that it was a collapsible bed – of a type much used in tenements to conserve space.

Fred and I sat on the edge of our beds, talking about the events of that dreary day and we both agreed that the future looked bleak. Fred declared, 'I'm not going to live in this place any longer than I have to!'

And so to bed on our first night in the wretched Avenue.

Chapter Eight

Fred and I lay in our beds and, in the flickering light of the two candles, scanned our surroundings. We lay at right angles, which meant that the foot of my bed was six inches from the side of his. I was lying with my feet towards him, and above my head was a small window set in the wooden wall, which separated the room from the outside passage.

It was soon apparent that we were going to have a far from peaceful sleep. I could hear the 'clump, clump' of feet on the stairs above our heads. I don't know how long before drowsiness began to overtake me, but in that mysterious world of semi-consciousness I heard my name called. I sat up and looked towards Fred, who, not looking at me, called my name again. 'What is it?' I asked, but he didn't answer, he just sat motionless, staring at a black object moving slowly up his arm. I gaped at what I then realised to be the granddaddy of those most loath-some of creatures – a huge cockroach!

It was obvious that Fred was so shocked that he was unable to lift his hand to knock it off. I scrambled along my bed and gave it an almighty swipe and then both of us yelled and fled into the kitchen.

Mother, who had just unfolded her collapsible bed, was startled by our hasty entry, but even more shocked when we told her the reason. She turned down Fred's blankets and, to our horror, we saw about half a dozen of

those obscenities, which began to scuttle over the edge
of the bed. Further examination revealed that both our
beds were 'alive', not only with beetles but also equally
repulsive bedbugs. (One of Granddad's pungent comments came to mind at that moment, 'The houses that
are empty are fit only for animals to live in.')

The shock of it all proved too much for Mother –
she sat on the table and sobbed bitterly. We two, equally
shocked, could only sit and watch her.

After recovering her composure, she decided that we
should sleep in her bed and she would rest on the couch.
But that dreadful experience was to be indelibly printed
on our minds, and I am sure it was one of the causes for
the change in Fred's temperament, because very soon his
cheerful grin and placid outlook were replaced by surliness and even open rebellion

To this day I wonder whether the constant arguments
between our parents, Dad's absence in the army and the
unpleasantness of that awful hovel, were the primary reasons for Fred's stammer – which had grown noticeably
worse.

Even at the early age of seven I had come to accept
that our future life in such deplorable surroundings
was to be a grim affair – how grim I was to learn only
too well.

Morning – and with it came an awakening in every
sense of the word. Sleep had come slowly and it wasn't
at all peaceful. It was one long nightmare punctuated by
the weeping of a very fretful baby Ethel.

It was bitterly cold, and we dressed hurriedly – a close
examination of our clothes ensured that there were no
bugs nestling in them. Mother, who had not bothered to
undress, attended to the baby as we kids struggled to light
a fire. When it was burning brightly Fred went to the sink
to fill the kettle, but when he reached it he recoiled with
a yell of disgust. 'Look at these,' he shouted. There were
more cockroaches trying to climb out of the sink.

Muttering angrily, Mother boiled the kettle and promptly poured the contents over the hateful things, which were then scooped up and burned on the fire. There was no other way of dealing with them.

After we had breakfasted, Mother left the house and returned a little later with her sister. Then began a period of feverish activity; our beds were dismantled, thoroughly scrutinised, then stacked in the kitchen. Holes and cracks were filled with plaster.

The whole operation was completed with a generous coating of creosote and liberal applications of bug powder.

While all that was in progress, Fred and I decided to take a walk around The Avenue.

What we saw defies adequate description. Without doubt those dwellings were relics from the Dickensian era.

The Avenue stretched from Elswick Road to Scotswood Road, and almost every house in it was tenemented. There were four courtyards and a conglomeration of passages. Situated at one end of each of these courtyards was a row of toilets, and we watched as queues formed outside each of them. We were soon to become accustomed to this distressing necessity.

It would be almost impossible to describe every aspect of this dirty lane, but this much can be said – even in those days of housing shortages and woeful sanitary facilities, the conditions that prevailed in The Avenue were almost beyond belief. The overcrowding can be better understood if I list the people who occupied our tenement: a family of six lived in two small basements; immediately above us – in two rooms – was a family of seven. At the rear, above, was another family of six, and at the rear of our room lived a family of four. A grand total of twenty-seven souls, most of whom were trying desperately to retain a little dignity in the face of those dreadful conditions. This was the general pattern in the area.

As we made our way home after our 'tour', Fred, with hope in his voice, said, 'We may not be living here very long, Mother expects a better place very soon.'

Dear God, how soon is very soon?

Chapter Nine

It is April 1915 and we were now in our fourth week of residence in The Avenue and Mother had made a tremendous effort to brighten up our lives. All cracks and holes had been filled in and treated with disinfectant, and the dirty old wallpaper had been replaced by new. It soon became obvious that such measures would have to be taken at regular intervals in order to keep the cockroaches at bay. Unfortunately, the treatment had no effect on the bedbugs, and they constantly plagued our lives.

During the weeks that followed we began to realise what life in The Avenue was all about.

First there had been the question of our education, and this had been promptly dealt with following a visit by the school board man. Sadly, I was not allowed to attend the same school as Fred; he had to enrol at Lefroy Street, while I was despatched to a Church School – St Nicholas.

It was now becoming distressingly obvious that we were to live in The Avenue indefinitely; Mother had made efforts to obtain a better house but the rents demanded were far beyond her means. She was, of course, receiving a weekly army allowance but it was a mere pittance, and as the weeks went by she was being forced more and more into using some of the money Dad had deposited in the post office when he had enlisted.

We now knew that this particular community was predominately a Catholic one; the minority were a mixture of Protestants, Wesleyans and various others. As so often happens when a variety of religions are packed together, there was constant friction between them.

It couldn't be doubted, in spite of the filth and vermin, that there were many people in this community who were proud and decent and whose daily life was a continuous battle against the frightful living conditions, but who, despite the odds against them, succeeded in retaining some dignity. Unfortunately, these people were very often the target of brutal physical and verbal attacks from the less respectable citizens of that rabbit-warren. It is so easy, after a space of time, to become engulfed by one's surroundings; to begin to take for granted, or accept as a way of life many things which had at first been nauseating. For instance, Fred and I were shocked when we first saw a procession of women walking down The Avenue in the morning towards the toilets – each with a full bucket. Perhaps there is nothing unusual about using buckets. It wouldn't have mattered had there been some means of disposing of the contents out of view of sniggering onlookers.

After a while, Fred and I ceased to be disgusted – we accepted it as a necessary evil. After all, didn't we have to do it too?

Accepting those parts of life as normal didn't mean that one had to like it – and I never did.

Trying to make friends among the young members of this community was something I hadn't even considered. I had witnessed the brutal attacks made by various boys on younger and weaker ones. I had listened to their vile language. But, as I was to discover later, there were other boys, who, like me, remained aloof from the savage fun of those young brutes. Oddly enough, Fred began to shed his inhibitions and mix freely with some lads of his age, particularly one by the name of Jack Allen.

I think it would be safe to say that Fred and I, while in no way losing our affection for each other, began to live separate lives from then on. He seldom sat indoors, but I, having developed a passion for reading, was quite content to do so and devour any kind of boys' books I could gather.

Which brings me to my entry into St Nicholas'. This was a remarkable school in many ways. It was situated in a most unlikely spot – almost directly beneath the High Level Bridge and right in the centre of a nondescript area called Hanover Square. It was difficult to imagine that this squat, dirty little building was, in fact, a school.

My first day as a pupil was quite an eventful one. We began, Mother and I, by failing to locate the blooming place. We were eventually directed, by a passer-by, along a narrow lane leading from a big railway arch at the foot of Westgate Road. We walked across a miniature play-yard, and when we entered I was understandably depressed.

First impressions can sometimes be wrong and so it proved in this instance. I was to learn that this school had mostly been occupied by the choristers of St Nicholas' Cathedral – a sort of school for music. Well, their heavenly warbling may have done little to enhance the exterior of the building, but the interior had absorbed the tranquillity and reverence which is the hallmark of such music.

After an interview with the Headmaster, Mr Robson, Mother took her leave and I was escorted to a classroom in which were seated about thirty boys and girls.

The teacher, Miss Winter, a forbidding looking woman in a long black dress, took me to a double desk and sat me down beside a girl my age.

You must forgive me for dwelling at length on my first day in this school; I do so because the next four years there proved to be very happy ones and that particular young girl was to become very dear to me – as you will learn later.

Chapter Ten

Such was the maze of passages and the siting of dwellings in the most unlikely of places in The Avenue, I am sure that had I lived in that area for the whole of my life there would still have been a host of troglodytes of whose existence I would never have known.

After almost three months, however, I knew most of the names of our immediate neighbours – and by God there were some real characters among them.

Incidentally, although I am going to describe their eccentricities, I am not going to give their real names – but the stories are true.

Take for instance the family who lived above us – a father, mother, three sons and two daughters. The children's ages ranged from eight to eighteen and yes, they all ate and slept in two rooms. They must have lived particularly miserable lives.

The mother was a habitual drunkard and the father (I'll call him Harry), who had steady employment, regularly came home from the pub during the weekend absolutely sloshed. (Oddly enough he didn't drink during the week.)

Immediately after his return from the pub there would begin an argy-bargy between him and his pickled wife, and their yells and screams would be heard for miles around, but no one ever took much notice of them. Neither did we – until one particular Saturday evening.

It was well after ten o'clock and Mother, Fred and I were having our supper when we heard the father fall into the passage. We listened as he crawled up the stairs and when we heard him bang on the door of his flat we prepared ourselves for the usual noisy argument. But this was a special night.

Seconds after he had entered we heard an unusual noise, like a reverberating 'CLUNK'. That was followed by an angry high-pitched yell from the mother. They began arguing, and Harry let out a screech of agony, which was followed by what sounded like people running. It continued for some minutes, during which time we noticed, with alarm, that our ceiling was moving up and down!

Then, to our astonishment, there followed a long series of heavy thumps. This proved too much of an ordeal for the gas-mantle, which gave a convulsive shudder and then disintegrated! Fred and I thought this was great fun but Ma was not amused. 'I'm not going to stand for this,' she yelled. (But apart from fitting a new mantle there was really nothing she could do.)

There came a lull in the proceedings, and naturally we thought the pantomime was over. Not a bit of it.

Harry continued to shout, and Fred said, 'I think he's shouting out of the window.' We went to the front door and looked up, and there he was, stripped to the waist, leaning out of the window and holding a small Union Jack in each hand. In a loud voice, full of defiance, he was saying over and over again, 'Balls the Pope, up the King!'

Now that was a dangerous utterance in any Catholic-dominated area, let alone The Avenue. Windows were hastily opened and outraged Catholics poked their heads out, looking for the instigator of this sacrilege. The pipe-smoking old hag two windows away put a damper on his royal fervour. 'Fuck off, John Bull's bastard,' she snarled. Fred and I discreetly withdrew.

The next morning there was a sequel to that episode. Like everyone else in the area we had a bucket in our room, but for the sake of hygiene we used ours only in an emergency, if there was any daylight at all we would make the journey to the toilet.

That's what I had done this particular morning. It was fairly early, about 8 a.m., and as I made my way back I heard the sound of a bell ringing in the distance. I looked down The Avenue and saw it was a milkman. I hadn't seen or heard this man before, so I stood for a while watching him clanging the bell, which was as big as a poss-stick!

Suddenly I heard a groan from above, and, looking up, I saw Harry, elbows on the windowsill and his head between his hands. He must have had a king-size hangover because he was groaning something terrible.

The milkman, with his small churn mounted on a wheelbarrow, was getting nearer and nearer. He was still ringing that bell non-stop. When he reached the front of our house I decided to go indoors; but then I heard a frantic yell. 'Hey you,' roared our upstairs neighbour.

'Me?' queried the milkman.

'Yes, you,' came the reply. 'Stop ringing that bloody bell or I will come down there and ram it up your bloody arse.'

The milkman looked at him for a moment. 'Very well,' he said, and moved away. As he did so Harry withdrew his head and closed the window.

The milkman had gone just a few yards when he stopped and looked up at the window. He came back to a spot directly under it, then, grasping the bell with both hands, and with a look of fiendish delight on his face, he began to swing the bronze monstrosity up and down at ever-increasing tempo. It was absolutely awful.

The effect on Harry must have been devastating. I heard him give an agonising yell as he opened his window and poked his head out – but he hurriedly withdrew it again. Very soon he resembled a bird in a cuckoo clock; every time he pushed his head out of the window the deafening clamour drove him back. Cheerfully unperturbed, Milko continued with his ruthless retaliation against the man who had threatened to distort his arsehole.

Relief finally came as window after window was violently opened and irate occupants shook their fists; threatening to make not only the bell disappear up Milko's arse – but the churn as well.

I later found out exactly what had happened the night the mantle collapsed from one of Harry's sons.

When Harry arrived home that night his wife was sitting – slightly cock-eyed – imbibing her favourite tipple. Harry lurched over to the sink, picked up an enamel dish and promptly 'crowned' her with it (that was the clunk we heard). She lunged at him with a pair of fire tongs and almost fractured his goolies (that was the agonising shriek). Then, on their hands and knees, they scrabbled after each other round and round the kitchen table. Eventually they stood at opposite ends of the table, jumping up and down, jabbering away like two demented chimpanzees (hence the broken gas mantle).

Chapter Eleven

'May I walk home with you?' Surprised, I turned and looked at the girl who had addressed me. 'Of course,' I said. Her name was Irene, and she was the girl I had sat next to on my first day at St Nicholas' (or St Nick's, as we called it).

This was my fourth week at the school and I now knew a little more about the place. It was a very small school by present-day standards. There were four small classrooms with an average of thirty pupils in each. There were only a few staff; the Head, Mr Robson, who dressed and acted like a genial farmer; twin sisters the Winters, who, despite their austere appearance, were kind and gentle ladies; and finally Mr Leech, the youngest of the four.

The idea of a boy and girl sitting together was the brainchild of one of the Winters ladies, and the object was to teach us how to behave in the presence of the opposite sex. (Some of the more precocious boys often took advantage of it!)

Irene was a cheerful girl, but during my first day at school I spoke only in monosyllables. I was a shy young lad in those days. Her father, like mine, was a miner and he too had enlisted in the army. She was an only child and lived with her mother in Maple Street, which was only a short distance from The Avenue.

I remember vividly her reaction when I turned into The Avenue after that first walk home. 'Do you live up there?' she asked. I nodded, whereupon she shook her head and wrinkled her nose. Eventually however, I began to meet her on the way to school, and except for a few short breaks, I continued to do so for the next four years.

Mother had received a letter from Dad and in it he expressed great concern for us having to live in this area. But once again there was no information as to his whereabouts.

Fred appeared to have shrugged off the worst of his sullen mood, but I noticed that he spent little time indoors.

Although I became more familiar with some young-sters of my age, I still remained somewhat aloof. This was partly due to an encounter with a bunch of evil young louts. I had to visit the toilet late one Saturday afternoon, and when I reached the wretched area I found about ten youths playing football – at least that's what I thought. I walked passed them and as I did so, the thing they were kicking landed at my feet. To my disgust I saw it wasn't a ball but a large rat – and it was still alive. I heard one of them shout, 'Kick it kidder,' but I ignored them and walked towards the toilet.

I was about to enter when I was suddenly grabbed from behind by two of the larger boys and rammed against the wall. Horrified, I saw that one of them was holding the almost-dead rat in his hand. 'Listen pansy,' he snarled, 'when I say kick it, kick it!' He flung it to the ground. 'Now, kick it,' he yelled, and raised his fist. I was absolutely petrified with fear and revulsion as I gazed at that awful rat. Somehow I wriggled free and fled back home, where I was uncontrollably sick.

I am not sure even now what shocked me more – the rat, or being called a pansy.

I told my story to Fred, then not quite ten years old, who declared, 'This place is a breeding ground for brutes like that, so you will have to steer clear of them. But there are some decent lads out there and you ought to mix with them. For goodness sake get yourself outdoors more and stop reading so much.'

The very next day I decided to join some boys who were playing 'mount-a-kitty', and it was then that my Avenue education really began.

I was standing at the front door, minding my own business as usual, when one of a group of boys called out to me, 'Warramanshort, wannaplay?' Remembering my experience of the previous day I looked up suspiciously, then shook my head. But he persisted, 'Howway man, yijussgorrastanaginawall?'

Well, even though I was aware that most of those boys were tearaways, I hadn't really seen them doing anything wrong, so I agreed to join them.

After the teams were picked I found myself standing with my back against a wall facing a human caterpillar. The head of the first boy was resting on my midriff and the following four were bent over behind each other. The object of it all was that four other boys would try and leap the full length of the said caterpillar. It was a strange game to me!

So there I stood, waiting innocently for the proceedings to begin. Those who were to jump had backed about twenty yards away, then, with some trepidation, I saw the first of them come hurtling towards us. He made a tremendous leap and whooshed through the air towards me – it scared me to death – so I sidestepped. All hell broke loose! The boy with his head on my stomach lost his grip and butted the wall, while the boys behind him lost their balance and fell to the ground. But the jumper, being unable to halt in mid-air, hit the wall face first with an unpleasant 'splat'.

With some dismay I looked at the boys who were cursing and spitting out vile language, but then the flier, who had bashed the wall, came towards me growling like an animal and with blood running profusely down his chin. He was about ten years old, but I was shocked to see such dreadful malevolence on his face.

Dear God, that young thug battered me with unbelievable savagery, with his hands and feet coming at me
from all directions. He was so intent on my total destruc-
tion that it took the combined efforts of two men to
drag him away from me. Battered, bleeding and sobbing
I just sat on the ground until Fred and Mother carried
me inside.

I learned later that my assailant was the leader of a
pack of vicious louts and had been congratulated by his
mother for 'doing a good job on me'!

There are lots of people in this world whom I dislike
intensely, but never have I nursed such hatred for anyone
that would remotely compare with my feelings towards
that boy. Forever afterwards I thought of him as 'Thug'.

Chapter Twelve

The injuries I received during that encounter were more extensive than was first thought. Closer examination revealed severe bruising to my body through being booted, a gash on the back of my head, and one of my front teeth had been knocked out.

Mother was so angry she decided to call in the police but her sister advised her not too. 'If you do that,' she said, 'the little brute's family will lead you a hell of a life.' It was decided the incident should be forgotten, but, and melodramatic though it may sound, I made a silent vow that someday I would exact retribution for that fearful beating.

Mother thought it better for me to stay away from school for a while but I persuaded her to let me return after only one day off. My young girl friend, Irene, was horrified and when she asked me what happened I replied, 'Oh, I got knocked down by a horse and cart.' (Well!) Even my teacher was greatly concerned. She gave me a packet of sweets and roundly condemned the fictitious horse and cart!

During June it became obvious to everyone that the war was to last much longer than we had anticipated, and the shape of things to come – at least in our household – was heralded when Mother warned us to take good care of our clothes because there would be little or no money to replace them.

She was becoming increasingly worried by baby Ethel's troublesome cough. The doctor had been called in twice and he had expressed concern about our living conditions, which he said were causing Ethel's illness.

There was no improvement in her condition after another week, so Mother took her to the children's hospital. They diagnosed bronchitis which they, too, blamed on our living conditions. The baby was admitted for a few days and when she returned there was a marked improvement in her condition, but sadly, within a very short time, the wretched cough returned.

Neither Fred nor I was aware of just how ill she was until one morning, when we both woke before dawn to sounds of great activity coming from the kitchen. We opened our room door and to our dismay we saw Mother nursing the baby and crying bitterly. Fred was about to ask what was wrong when Bella came hurrying in. 'The doctor is on his way,' she said to Mother.

We left the kitchen when the doctor arrived but remained standing near the open door of our room. Fred listened closely to what the doctor was saying then sat on the bed alongside me. 'Ethel must be very ill,' he said, 'because I heard him tell Mother to send for our father.'

It came as a dreadful shock to learn that our little sister was critically ill. She was just nine months old, and even after so many years I can still vividly remember every small detail, every harrowing moment after the doctor gave the dreadful news.

Mother insisted that we both went to Bella's until it was time to go to school, and so, for the first time, we stood in her house among a brood of scruffy little girls. It was a relief to both of us when we left, although neither of us felt inclined to go to school.

I didn't wait for my friend Irene when the dinner bell rang, but hurried home on my own. The events of the morning were still fresh in my mind, but truth to tell I was more interested in whether my father had arrived home.

I stood for a few moments just inside the kitchen door looking at the dark drape that completely covered the window, and, young though I was, I knew what it meant. Then I was clasped in the strong arms of my father.

On a glorious summer afternoon, Mother, Fred and I sat in a horse-drawn coach with the mortal remains of our young sister lying in a glass case fitted to the rear of it, as we made our melancholy journey to the cemetery. Etched deeply on my mind is the memory of Dad, stern faced but erect, as he walked alone behind the coach.

He had been granted five days leave, which meant he had to return when the funeral was over, but he seemed too upset to spend time with or talk much to us boys. We could sense he was shaken, not only by the death of the baby but also by our living conditions, which he was seeing for the first time. We had seen his pursed lips and his expression of disbelief when he had looked into our box-room, but he said nothing about it to us. He returned to his unit looking like a changed man.

Many times during the weeks that followed, Mother would cry and then ask, 'Would the baby have lived if we had remained at Ashington?' Well, Fred and I asked the same question many times, but of course there was no answer. Nevertheless, the hideous reality of life in The Avenue had been brought home to us. We also realised that simply keeping ourselves and our rooms as clean as possible was no defence against the germ-infested atmosphere in which we were living.

It was ironic, however, that the tragic death of the baby should lead me to form my first friendship with two Avenue boys.

A good lady, Mrs Peters, who lived in a tenement next to ours, called in to offer her condolences. She must have realised the difficulties we were in. It was out of the question for anyone to sleep in the kitchen with the baby lying in her pathetically small coffin in the centre of the floor, so she offered to take Fred and me until the funeral was over.

Fred, however, decided to stay with his friend Jack, so for a few days I slept in a bed alongside Mrs Peter's two sons, Bob and George. It was the beginning of a friendship that was to last for many years.

Chapter Thirteen

We learned later that Ethel had died from diphtheria, which, in those days, was a scourge among children and all too often fatal.

Looking back on that unhappy week, what struck me most forcibly was the apparent indifference of most of The Avenue populace to our bereavement. As time went by, however, I realised that this was nothing unusual. The festering sore in which we all lived, with its damp, vermin-infested houses and primitive sanitary arrangements, was a breeding ground for killer diseases such as tuberculosis and bronchitis. As a consequence, the death rate in the area was appallingly high and seldom a week passed without a funeral in the neighbourhood. To most people in that place, death was unremarkable, and the regular gruesome visits by those dreary horse-drawn hearses left them completely unmoved.

It soon became painfully obvious that our financial position was in a precarious state, as was Mother's state of mind. Very wisely she took a job in a small-arms factory, which not only helped to lift her depression but also improved our living standards.

As time passed, the shock of the baby's death began to recede and I was spending a little more time outdoors with my new friends, but I still found time to indulge in my favourite hobby – reading.

I think it was about that time that I learned another lesson on life in The Avenue.

It was a very hot, humid Saturday evening, just before my eighth birthday. Most residents had opened their windows to allow what passed for fresh air into their houses.

Playing football in the streets was a popular pastime, but any kind of rubber ball was a luxury so the boys had to improvise, and the grisly ingenuity of some of them was amazing. They would simply steal a sheep or pig's bladder from a slaughterhouse, part fill it with water and inflate it with air. That Saturday excitement was running high as they booted the bladder in all directions – until one of them gave it an extra hearty wallop. The thing sailed through the air and at the same moment Mrs McNally, a notorious Irish troublemaker, leaned out of her open window and received the full impact of the bladder, square in the mush. If that wasn't enough, the damn bladder burst and the slimy contents trickled down her face!

With an ear-shattering scream of rage, she raced out of the house clutching the sorry remains of the missile. Swearing violently she grabbed the youth who had belted it and proceeded to choke him by pushing that dirty piece of offal down his throat. Then all hell broke loose.

The unfortunate boy, glassy-eyed and horror-stricken, promptly fainted. His outraged mother, a hefty woman, came charging up The Avenue and grabbed the screaming Irishwoman. Within seconds those two members of the fair sex were rolling on the ground, snarling, clawing and kicking each other, like two bloody alley cats!

Then the fathers decided to knock the daylights out of each other. I watched open-mouthed as brothers and sisters, uncles and aunts got stuck into their counterparts. Very soon it became a free for all.

A variety of missiles began flying through the air: pokers, flat irons and even pots and pans. The frequent screams of agony, together with the constant swearing, was awe-inspiring. I thought those vicious snarling savages would have eaten each other if they could!

The arrival of a posse of policemen eventually put an end to the show, and when the combatants – those who could – scuttled back to their homes, they left behind a fearsome collection of weapons and casualties.

Watching that fracas had a profoundly depressing effect on me, and I wondered with dismay whether such scenes were a popular pastime in The Avenue (they were!). But even the most serious of situations has a lighter side – this one certainly did.

The following morning we saw one of the men who had taken part in the attempted genocide – a man called Joe L. – carefully scrutinising the cobbles on the spot where the fight had taken place. His head and face were swathed in bandages, and when asked what he was looking for, he replied in an aggrieved tone, 'I was only trying to calm everybody down, and do you know what some dirty bugger went and done, eh?' He paused, then almost in tears said, 'Chewed my fuckin' lug off, that's what!'

'Sam,' shouted Mother, 'Go outside and see if you can find a decent poker!'

Chapter Fourteen

At the end of July we received a letter from Dad telling us he was coming home on a short leave. By a cruel twist of fate it was the same day our good friend, Mrs Peters, received the dreaded notification that her husband had been killed in action. Two days later another lady, who lived above us at the rear, was informed that she too had lost her husband.

I have always considered it remarkable that The Avenue, despite its notorious reputation, lost so many of its menfolk during the Great War. They enthusiastically volunteered to defend a country which had treated them like scum in peacetime.

News of casualties in friends' families was having a bad effect on Mother and we two kids. Mother said it would probably be Dad's last leave before going overseas – and into battle.

An invitation to my friend Irene's birthday party was a welcome distraction. She and I were by then very close friends, yet I would not have taken her to my home (and I doubt whether her mother would have approved of my exposing her to the sneers and catcalls of some of my neighbours). One week after the party, I waited for her at our usual meeting place – at the bottom of Rye Hill – but she didn't turn up, and although I was puzzled I had to gallop off to school on my own. My teacher told me that Irene was absent because her father had been killed at the front. I could not have been more shocked had it have been my own father.

Dad arrived looking smart and bronzed, but once again there arose the question of sleeping accommodation. Mrs Peters, once again, provided me with a bed and Fred slept with his friend Jack, but I couldn't help wondering what was to happen when Dad returned home permanently.

As the shock of Ethel's death became more distant, Dad began taking stock of our living conditions, and, to put it mildly, he became very angry. So upset was he that within an hour of his arrival he and Mother had a right 'up and downer'. (The answer to his question 'Why did you come here in the first place?' was not forthcoming until years later.)

My circle of friends was increasing rapidly, thanks to my association with Bob and George. I now knew Billy, Jimmy, Percy, Susan, Rose and Agatha. We always played in the nearby parks because had we felt inclined to run around The Avenue – which we never did – we would have had to endure the unwelcome attentions of Thug and his gang of toughs. They ruled that particular roost and woe-betide any misguided youths who thought otherwise.

I had often noticed a lad – sometimes barefooted – watching us whilst we played. I got the impression he would have liked to have joined in the fun, but he always confined himself to looking on. He seemed lonely, as though he wanted to be friendly with everyone but didn't know how to go about it.

One afternoon I was returning from the butchers with the meat for our dinner (half a pound of sausage) and I saw the lad being attacked by the neighbourhood toughs. He was barefooted and his tormentors had formed a ring around him. There was a flurry of blows as Thug, backed by yells of 'kill him' from his cronies, began a ferocious attack. Shoeless or not, the lad had no intention of going down without a fight. Thug began to kick the bare feet of his luckless opponent his pals joined in, and very soon the battered lad fell to the ground. I could only stand and watch.

The boy was helped to his feet by some outraged women, and as they were cleaning him up I heard someone say, 'Poor old muck, always in trouble.' The victim looked at the mob who had hammered him and said defiantly, 'I will get you for this – every fuckin' one of you.'

Later I learned that the boy's name (or nickname) was Muck! Muck kept his promise; over time and one-by-one he belted the living daylights out of every one of his attackers, including Thug.

Chapter Fifteen

The year 1916 was well into its stride but there was little to cheer about in The Avenue. Even the coming of summer did little to lift our spirits.

Of course the growing list of war casualties did not help, and the monthly *Gazette*, which published the names of the dead and wounded, was anxiously perused by everyone.

Mother continued to work at the arms factory, and our finances, though not opulent, paid for a reasonable standard of living. She had also tried very hard to find a better house, but without success. I was sure that at last she had accepted the inevitable – that only a miracle would get us out of The Avenue, where we had already lived for more than a year.

Mother was beginning to worry a great deal about Dad. It had been three months since his last letter to her, and because his address was that of an army post office, there was no way of knowing where he was. Her fears that he was in action were increased when she at last received a field postcard stating only 'that he was well'.

As if we hadn't had enough troubles, fate had a nasty surprise for my dear brother.

Fred was a great one for running. No matter where he was going to or coming from he always ran at top speed. Because of this, Mother didn't take much notice when he came home from school one afternoon complaining of a pain in his side. She dismissed it as a stitch and he returned to school for the afternoon session. Just an hour later he was brought back by his teacher – the pain in his side had worsened and he was having difficulty breathing.

Mother called a doctor immediately. It was the same one who attended Ethel, and he again condemned our living conditions as the primary cause of Fred's illness.

His diagnosis was swift and his reactions equally so. Within the hour Fred was admitted to the Fleming Hospital, dangerously ill with pleurisy.

For some days his condition was critical and Mother had been advised (again) to try and contact Dad. The authorities were sympathetic but unhelpful – leave could not be arranged. (We found out later that they were not lying.)

Some very anxious weeks followed before Fred, very slowly, began to turn the corner. The doctors told Mother to expect him to stay in hospital for a long time.

But there was yet more anxiety to come in the weeks that lay ahead. Mother was expecting another baby, and from conversations I overheard I understood there was the possibility that Mother would have to go to hospital. This was a frightening thought because it meant I would be alone.

Mother's sister Bella had taken over the running of our home and I was very, very unhappy. Then I discovered that no matter whether Mother had the baby at home or in hospital, I wouldn't be allowed to stay in the house on my own, which meant having to sleep at Bella's place.

This thought filled me with trepidation, because even with Mother around Bella made her dislike of me painfully apparent. She admitted she didn't like me and called me a cheeky little bugger.

Eventually, Mother decided – against the doctor's advice – to have the baby at home, and I was spared the nightmare of sleeping at Bella's by the generosity of Mrs Peters, who once again took me in. However, being hoofed out of my own home on a regular basis was beginning to unsettle me a great deal. If I had to be sent elsewhere every time an emergency came along what kind of life had I to look forward to?

As was normal at the time, I knew nothing about what happened during Mother's long confinement, and it was very much later before I was to learn that she had had a difficult time. Bella was a tower of strength, apparently.

But trouble hadn't finished with us. A few months after the birth of my new brother, Jim, we heard a rumour that a particular battalion of the Northumberland Fusiliers had been in action and there had been heavy casualties. It was impossible to get any official information, so the anxious families could only wait and pray.

Mother had almost recovered from the birth when, towards the end of the year, numerous telegrams were delivered to neighbours containing the awful notification of death in action. When we learned that the casualties were from Dad's battalion, Mother had a relapse. Once again Bella looked after her. Many weary, anxious days followed, during which every knock on the door made us tremble with fear.

Our agony was finally ended by Mrs Peters, who rushed in clutching the latest edition of the *Gazette*, and in it we saw, in cold, dispassionate print: PTE. S.W. Herbert. WOUNDED IN ACTION.

Chapter Sixteen

The official notification from the army regarding Dad didn't arrive until many weeks after we had read about him in the local paper. It told us nothing new. But the news was the tonic Mother needed.

Fred was still in hospital and I have to admit that I missed him tremendously, especially when I lay in bed in that dammed box-room without him for company. His absence also meant that I was all alone when I had a terrifying experience that left me shocked for a long time afterwards.

Fred had often spoken to me about a strange shuffling noise, which appeared to come from the staircase above our heads, usually in the dead of night. There were about twenty people living above us and there was a continual thump, thump of footsteps on the stairs, but Fred insisted that the noise he heard sounded as if something was being dragged up and down them. I had never heard the odd noise so I thought nothing of it – until about a month after Fred went into hospital.

Since our horrible experience with the cockroaches, Mother had bought a small paraffin lamp, which was kept burning during the night to discourage them.

One night I woke with a start in the early hours and, to my dismay, I saw the lamp had snuffed it and I was in complete darkness. I didn't worry unduly about that, but what did concern me was the likelihood of beetles crawling on the bed. I sat up and as I groped for the matches I heard an odd noise above me on the stairs. It sounded as though someone was pulling a bag of hay. It was then I remembered the strange sounds heard by Fred.

I stayed still for a few minutes until the noise ceased, but then I noticed a faint glow shining through the small window above my head. That meant someone had opened the front door, letting in the glow from the street lamp opposite.

I couldn't find the matches and I was about to grope my way into the kitchen when I heard the sound of a light being struck and saw a flickering reflection through the window – someone was standing in the passage.

There was nothing very mysterious about a person standing in the passage. Wasn't it possible that one of the upstairs tenants couldn't sleep and had come down to spend a few minutes at the front door? Nevertheless, I thought I would take a look.

I stood on the bed and, very carefully, lifted the hinged window and looked out. There was a man standing at the door, smoking a pipe. He had his back to me. His pipe must have gone out because he turned inwards and struck another match. While he held the flame to the pipe he looked upwards, and then my blood ran cold. Even by the flickering glare of the match I saw, to my horror, the hideous features of a gargoyle with just a cavity where the nose should have been, the side of the face puckered and twisted into a beastial snarl. I was so shocked I fell backwards on to the bed and then rolled on to the floor. Of course the din woke Mother, who hurried into the room with a candle and saw me sitting on the floor. 'What the devil is wrong with you?' she asked. I mumbled something about a funny-looking man standing in the passage. 'You must have had a nightmare,' she retorted. 'Go back to sleep, it is only three o'clock in the morning.'

Next morning I tried to explain to Mother what I had seen, but she pooh-poohed and said I was very definitely imagining things. And there the matter ended – at least for a while.

After many more anxious weeks, Mother at last received a letter from Dad, saying that he was in a military hospital somewhere in England and was hoping to be transferred to one nearer home. There was also better news about Fred, who was at last making satisfactory progress. However, Mother was very concerned about our finances. She had been unable to resume working at the arms factory and the money Dad had deposited in the post office had all gone. Her only income was her small army allowance, and it soon became apparent that she would have to suffer the dreaded indignity of applying to the hated parish for relief.

At least I had an abundance of decent clothes – Irene's mother had thoughtfully collected a huge bundle of clothes from her sister, whose two sons had outgrown them. I often wondered why she was so keen to see me well dressed. I was sure it was because she had no intention of allowing her smart, pretty daughter to be seen in the company of a lad with the arse of his trousers patched!

Near the end of the year we had a letter from Dad telling us he would be home for a spell of sick-leave before going into hospital near Newcastle. More than a year had passed since we had last seen him and we were thrilled at the prospect of having him home again. Unfortunately there was nothing Mother could do about our living conditions, and I had the unhappy feeling that I would be sleeping out again – at least for a while anyway.

Our pleasure was short-lived, however, because another letter came from Dad, saying that he would not, after all, be allowed to come home until he had been admitted to a hospital somewhere in Durham.

During the long weeks Fred had been in hospital, I had not been allowed to visit him – in fact Mother was allowed to see him only twice a week. (In those days patients were given a number, and each evening the numbers were published in the local paper under headings indicating the condition of the patients.) As a special concession however, I was eventually allowed to accompany Mother on one of her visits – and how I looked forward to seeing my brother again!

It wasn't a happy visit because we found Fred right down in the dumps. Doctors had discovered that fluid was once again forming in his lung. His hopes of being discharged before Dad arrived home had been cruelly shattered. I had never seen him so upset.

Mother had at last learned the exact day on which Dad would arrive home. The kitchen had been re-papered and painted by courtesy of a ticket from Todd Brothers on Scotswood Road. (I don't think they ever got their money!)

Dad had been transferred to the hospital in Durham, and after visiting him Mother knew more about his wounds and how he had come by them. It was obvious then why he couldn't be granted leave when Fred was taken ill. He was taking part in the ill-fated attempt to land on and take control of the Dardanelles. His hand was shattered and he had an open wound along his scalp. I was a little puzzled to hear Mother say to her sister, 'He has changed so much I hardly know him.'

The day we had looked forward to for so long at last arrived, and as a special treat Mother agreed to my accompanying her to the station to meet him. Numerous trains were arriving and disgorging all manner of servicemen and Mother searched anxiously among the milling crowd at the gates. Suddenly she walked quickly to the barrier and took the arm of a soldier – I say that because I failed to recognise my own father!

He had been twenty-six years old when he enlisted, but the man Mother was talking to looked twice that age. His moustache had been shaved off, his face was pale and drawn and his uniform was badly crumpled. I wondered what had happened to that smart soldier of the previous year.

Mother pointed me out to him, but he didn't have a welcoming smile for me, just a perfunctory pat on my head as he walked past. I remembered Mother's words to her sister – 'I barely know him' – and I began to under-stand why. For the moment anyway he was a complete stranger. After having waited with eager anticipation for so long to see him again, I felt miserable and deflated by his odd manner.

He barely spoke as we made our way home and even the 'welcome home' greetings from a few of the neighbours failed to elicit more than a curt nod in acknowledgement.

He became a little more relaxed as he sat on the couch along with Granddad, who had taken time off work to greet him. He declined to eat anything and after a short period he expressed a desire to catch up on some sleep.

Obviously the small celebration Mother had planned would have to be deferred. When Dad retired to the box-room he left behind a worried Mother, a perplexed Granddad and an unhappy little boy to whom he had not spoken a single word. His demeanour changed little during the six days he was with us, but he did visit Fred every day and at last remembered that he had a nine-year-old son and a new baby too.

My fears concerning the sleeping arrangements were fully confirmed, and with some disgust I learned that I would have to sleep at Bella's – 'just for the week', as Mother put it. I was absolutely shattered when Bella took me upstairs, where her brood were already con-gregated. There were seven of them – six girls and a boy – but I could only see two beds. She pointed to one of them; 'There are only three in that bed so you can sleep at the bottom.' (If you are wondering why I didn't sleep with George and Bob the answer is they had relatives staying with them.)

I was acutely embarrassed when I began to undress because I'd never had to do so in the presence of girls. Those giggling brats were none too bashful – a bare bum to them was simply a bare bum. Eventually I found myself tucked in with the boy at one end of the bed, and two of the girls at the other. It was a nightmare! I awoke, gasping for breath, to find a foot pressing on my throat, and then I began to scratch incessantly (fleas!). Before dawn broke I had been kicked, punched, scratched and rolled on, and the final indignity, I was peed on by someone with a gargantuan bladder!

As wrathful as any young boy could be, I raced home just before breakfast and startled Mother by stripping off and handing her my shirt, which by then was emitting a fearsome pong.

To my great relief it was decided that I would sleep in my own home, on the settee.

Shortly after Dad returned to the hospital, Fred arrived home, to my great delight. Pleurisy had left him with a troublesome cough, but despite that and the pain he suffered for almost a year, his cheery grin soon returned.

It became painfully obvious how pitifully inadequate our home would be when Dad returned for good. There would be five of us living, eating and washing in one room, and because there was only a tiny box-room, Dad and Mother would have to sleep in the kitchen.

I was soon to understand why many of the boys – and girls – who lived in The Avenue looked upon sex simply as a topic for lewd conversations – they were so used to witnessing sexual activity in their midst. In fairness to Mother, I must say that she was well aware of the problems that lay ahead and had made frantic efforts to obtain better and more commodious accommodation, but as before, there was nothing doing.

The main sufferer was Fred who needed plenty of fresh air and good solid food to build him up again, but neither of those vital commodities was available. It was noticeable how rebellious he had become over our appalling living conditions, and even though he was only twelve years old, there was a marked coolness against Mother in almost every action. There was no doubt he bitterly resented her moving us to The Avenue, and he didn't hesitate to say so on numerous occasions. After all, wasn't the move responsible for the death of the baby and his own serious illness? I hated the place just as much as he did, but I understood that no matter who was to blame, we would have to stay there for the foreseeable future.

I was rather startled by something Fred said one evening as we sat on our beds. First he asked me, 'Do you remember Mother leaving us with the baby when we were at Ashington, and hurrying off to Newcastle after she had received a letter.' I remembered the day perfectly. 'Well,' he went on, 'When she came back home she looked as if she had been crying, so I wondered whether it had been something to do with this house.' He didn't talk about this again, but after many years I learnt just how perceptive he was.

Our only hope was that Dad would manage to make some improvement in our living conditions when he was discharged from the army. He had had two operations on his hand but sadly it seemed as if he would be left permanently disabled.

The year 1917 was drawing to a close, but the conflict in Europe continued with unabated fury and it had become necessary to introduce rationing. It was a blow to many people but it didn't affect us – we were already on the breadline.

My happiest times were when I was at school. Irene and I had become firm friends and most Sunday afternoons I would be invited to tea with her and her mother. I was sure that her mother still harboured some reservations about our friendship. After all, wasn't I an Avenue dweller? I became more and more ashamed of living in that area; it was notorious and outsiders thought that everyone who lived there was the same. I was no angel – my pals and I got up to as much mischief as any other boys, but I think Irene's mother tolerated me because I kept myself clean and didn't speak in broad Geordie.

School was quite a way from home and some pupils had even longer distances to travel than I did. During bad weather many of us would arrive absolutely soaked. The staff decided to do something about it. And what they did was brilliantly simple. Each pupil was asked to bring to school one vegetable and a penny (I had to take a spud.) The pennies were used to buy bones from a curing factory. The school caretaker and a team of local ladies used these ingredients to make broth, so that we could have our lunch at school. That meant of course making only two journeys a day instead of four. In the winter months we could stay warm and snug indoors with warm, nutritious food to eat.

On days when no broth was available, we went to the corner shop opposite the school, where three half pence would buy a small pie and a 'paper' of lovely hot mashed potatoes.

Remember the boy whose name was Muck, who had been so badly beaten up by the local toughs? It was about that time I encountered him again. I was standing at our front door watching him being dragged along the pavement on an old sack, when he suddenly emitted an ear-piercing shriek and leaped high into the air – and the sack followed him! He groped frantically at his backside, but when the awful truth dawned he began to babble hysterically, 'I'm stuck, I'm stuck to a fuckin' sack!' I hurried over to him and when I looked at him it became obvious what had happened. His backside had been skewered by a massive nail and was now firmly attached to a dirty old coal sack!

A group of spectators quickly gathered and made facetious comments, which only added to the lad's misery. It was only after some time had elapsed that someone carefully cut away the bag and carted poor Muck off to the Infirmary to have the spike removed. That was the day I learned his full name, Terence Muckian.

Chapter Seventeen

I have had many experiences dealing with all kinds of people, including screwballs and nutcases, but I never encountered such a complex character as that boy called Muckian.

Since the nail-in-the-backside incident he had begun to tag along with me and my friends.

Bobby and George were not too keen though because Muckian did have a bit of a 'record'. He frequently played 'hookey' from school and often absented himself from home – sometimes for more than a week. He did own footwear but he preferred to run about barefooted. But bare feet were not an uncommon sight in those days. What was it that drew us together? Certainly not first impressions, because years after, when we asked each other that question, he said, 'I used to think you were a toffee-nosed twat!'

I thought he was a scruffy sod!

But the more he ran around with us the more I began to understand him. I learned that he was one of four brothers, who were not averse to belting him on the slightest pretext. After the beatings he would run away.

He was a squat boy – much shorter than I, even though he was two years older, and he was surprisingly shy. He could be generous to a fault, hated dishonesty, and had an instinctive love for animals. It wasn't unusual to see him standing at the street corner surrounded by dozens of mangy tom cats, who had been lured by his incredible imitation of a randy she-cat. He was absolutely fearless when dealing with dogs, especially the untrained snarling curs that dwelt in The Avenue. But he was terrified of girls. Should one of our Avenue girls approach us for a chat, he would promptly walk away. He used a lot of foul language and that was something I couldn't stand. But I blamed his home life – or lack of it – for that dreadful habit. The more time we spent with him, the more we began to realise that he sincerely wanted to lose his bad reputation. However, it was a long time before he realised that he had to work for what he wanted from life.

★ ★ ★

Christmas 1917 was a dreary affair, just like the others that we had spent in The Avenue. Mother was struggling to provide the bare necessities of life, so plum pudding and mince pies were an unobtainable dream.

Depressing as our circumstances were, the change in Dad was even worse. Gone was the good-tempered man we once knew; he had turned into an irascible, hard-swearing, heavy-drinking man, and he and Ma frequently had slanging matches.

Dad was spending most of his time at home pending his discharge from the army, and because of the enforced idleness he succumbed to the offers of 'have one on me' from well-meaning sympathisers. Unfortunately, as so often happens, he began to develop a taste for alcohol. On the other hand, he went berserk when my friend Billy's mother, well aware of our desperate circumstances, called at the house with a box of Christmas fare. 'I do not need charity from anyone,' he stormed.

Of course we were too young to understand the reasons for the changes in Dad, but with hindsight it is easier to see what he was going through. First and foremost was his disability, which had prevented him from resuming his career in the mines. It must have been a cruel blow to him. Then there was the hideous memory of taking part in one of the war's biggest disasters, the attempted storming of the Dardenelles, and the massacre of hundreds of his comrades. (Many times Fred and I were woken in the night by Dad's anguished cries as he relived the dreadful hours of that infamous action.) He had lost a daughter and almost lost a son. The home he had worked so hard for at Ashington had been replaced by a one-room hovel in a disreputable slum.

At twenty-nine, Dad was penniless, partially crippled, out of work and having to suffer humiliation at the hands of the supercilious bastards who manned the Parish Relief offices, in order to obtain a little cash and food vouchers. No wonder his natural dignity and pride had crumbled.

I know that quite a number of people who had lost loved ones in the forces considered that he was lucky to be home and out of it altogether. But what constitutes luck? In one way Dad was lucky – he came back. But is a man lucky to find himself crippled and plagued by dreadful nightmares? My Father himself answered that question during one particular period of depression, when he said, 'I was unlucky, the bullet that scalped me was half an inch too high.'

Because of our desperate situation, Mother began charring – our meagre income had to be supplemented somehow, otherwise we would have starved. In those days charring was a really thankless job. Because of their straitened circumstances, many women, like Mother, would travel as far afield as Gosforth and then do about six hours bloody hard work for the princely sum of six-pence an hour (and no travelling expenses).

It has to be remembered that half-a-crown would purchase bread, marge, tea, sugar, vegetables, and, with a bit of luck, a fourpenny parcel of meat scraps from the local butcher.

Mother soon had to give up charring though – she had to prepare herself for the arrival of another young Herbert!

It was about that time when a new dimension in my life was opened up – one that was to play a significant part in the years that lay ahead.

It all began at St Nick's during a music lesson. Without being conceited, I was aware that I had a good singing voice, and I used to enjoy the musical interludes. Judge my dismay, however, when the teacher, Miss Winter, dragged me to the front of the class and asked me to sing a verse from an old Scottish ballad. I tried to make excuses, but she would have none of it – 'I want you to show those corncrakes how to sing.'

She plonked her backside on the piano stool and depressed a key. 'Sing,' she ordered. So off I went with 'Ye Banks and Braes O' Bonny Doon, How Can Ye Bloom See Fresh and Fair,' I could swear that half the class were in tears when I finished! I suppose I was looking rather coy when I returned to my seat.

Our scripture lessons were given by a priest from the cathedral, and they always began by singing a hymn. For this particular lesson the chosen hymn was 'Jesus wants me for a sunbeam'. In view of what happened next, it was obvious that Miss Winter had been having a quiet word with the priest, because damn me if he didn't yank me to the front of the class and order me to sing the first verse! Well, children do not argue with priests, so off I went on my second solo effort.

The priest nodded his approval, and then he shocked me by saying, 'Why don't you join the cathedral choir? We'll teach you how to read music and give you training in singing.'

I was absolutely stunned! Me, in a choir? I returned a firm and decisive 'No.'

'You have a splendid voice.'

'I am sorry, Sir.'

'Think it over.'

'Yes, Sir.'

I had no intention of thinking anything over. Life in The Avenue was savage enough without the sneers and cat-calls that would surely come once it become known that I was a choirboy. No thank you very much. But I wasn't to escape so easily.

I decided not to mention the matter to Mother (Dad had returned to hospital for a final operation on his hand) and I fervently hoped I wouldn't hear any more about it.

But then Mr Robson, the Headmaster, tried to persuade me to join the choir. 'It would be a great honour,' he said. Even my young friend Irene tried hard to make me change my mind, but I still refused. I was aware that my teachers were rather put out, but they didn't live in The Avenue, did they?

A week went by without it being mentioned again, so I happily presumed that the matter was forgotten and in the past.

On the Sunday morning, however, there came a knock on our door, and when Mother opened it she must have been astonished to see a priest standing there.

'Mrs Herbert?'

'Yes.'

'I am the vicar of St Mary's Church.'

My heart sank because I recognised the voice – it was the priest who had tried to persuade me to join the choir!

'Is your son Samuel at home?'

'Yes,' answered Mother, then she turned to me. 'What have you been up to?' she bawled. The parson quickly assured her that I had done nothing wrong and then explained the reason for his visit. He had taken over the duties of the vicar, who was ill, and discovered that the choir was in great need of boy singers. He told Mother that I had refused to join the cathedral choir but maybe I would like to join that of the local church.

One thing I remember about that young priest – his self-control was superb when a stuffy old hag passed the door and shouted, 'Only fuckin' sinners need priests!' (But I never again saw him in The Avenue!)

I almost groaned out loud when Mother – without as much as a by-your-leave – answered for me, 'Yes, of course he will join the choir; it will keep him out of trouble.'

'When can I expect him?' asked the priest.

'I can send him along right away,' answered my helpful Mother. I was absolutely furious! Furious or not, just one and a half hours later, I found myself robed in a cassock and surplice, walking with the choir of St Mary's from the vestry to the pews, and in front of a huge congregation.

I was to become very familiar with that ritual during the following six years.

Chapter Eighteen

The year 1918 continued to drag on wearily. The latest addition to our family (Dora) had arrived, which created further problems in view of the limited accommodation. There were now six of us, living in conditions that could only be described as appalling – even in those days of acute housing problems.

Dad's final operation was partially successful, giving him limited use of his hand. He had been discharged from the forces and awarded a woefully inadequate disability pension.

Consequently, bread and margarine was our staple diet.

Unfortunately, Fred was the main sufferer. The lack of decent nourishing food was having a devastating effect on his health. He had resumed his schooling, but he was pale and drawn, and the constant racking cough – a legacy from his illness – was making his life almost unbearable.

I don't think I ever thanked my lucky stars for keeping me free from any kind of illness – but I should have done, because apart from minor ailments common to children, I had never suffered even a cold. I have to admit, however, that I collected more than a fair share of bruises when out gallivanting with my pals.

If anything could be called good during those desperate times, it would be the improvement in Dad. It seemed as though he had begun to accept the inevitability of having to start life afresh. He was also being a little more philosophical regarding his injured hand – but most important of all, he realised that he had four children who needed to be fed and clothed.

Proof of his new positive outlook came after he had gone to Ashington to find out if there was any possibility of obtaining employment at his former colliery. Sadly, because of his injured hand, there was nothing they could do for him. Then, at some cost to his dignity, he went from one council office to another, demanding a larger house and assistance towards our welfare. Well, he never did get a house, but the powers that be promised to send him on a rehabilitation course, and with that he had to be content.

In the meantime, Mother had decided to take in washing, which meant a twice-weekly journey for Fred and me to Jesmond, or even Gosforth. We would collect the clothes on a Monday and return them on a Saturday morning. But a lot used to happen during those four days!

She would wash and iron the clothes on the Tuesday. By Wednesday they were snugly ensconced in the local pawnshop. I often wondered what the owners' reactions would have been had they learned that their lovely white shirts were rubbing elbows with 'nitty' clothing in a backstreet pawnshop. Fred once said to Mother, 'You will be in the soup if the pawnshop should catch fire!'

Armistice Day arrived with its exaggerated celebrations. With all those millions of dead, one wondered what the hell there was to cheer about.

I was now in my eleventh year – three of which had been spent in The Avenue. Unbelievable!

Despite my initial reservations about joining the church choir, I found I really enjoyed it – even though I had to endure the bully boys' sneers, as I'd expected. Of course, Thug was the worst.

My father had become aware of the hatred I felt for that bully, and he gave me a stern lecture. 'You will never,' he began, 'indulge in any street brawls with that boy. No doubt the time will come when you will settle the account, but try and do it in a manly way. If singing in the choir is causing you too much embarrassment then pack it in.'

Well I had no intention of packing it in. Even though I didn't want to join in the first place, I had discovered that being a member of a choir comprising of twenty-six men and boys, leading a vast congregation in worship, gave me a feeling of achievement. When I was inside the church I was in a different world; gone was the squalor, the vermin, the foul language and the interminable street battles. There was a serene calmness and an atmosphere that would surely soothe the most troubled mind. As if by instinct, I became aware that the church had something to offer me – even if it was intangible.

On the earthly side, I had the added pleasure of knowing that my friend Irene and her mother worshipped there. Irene, by the way, was developing into a very pretty girl, and though her mother guarded her carefully, she never objected to our friendship. (Well, choirboys can do no wrong, can they?)

As it happened, we were both in our last few months at St Nick's because pupils were transferred to other schools on reaching the age of twelve, and I was a little sad that we would be going different ways. Irene just said, 'Let's wait and see what happens.'

My wayward pal Terence (Terry) Muckian was in the wars again. I was surprised to learn that he had done another bunk from home, because he had avoided trouble since he started going around with us. Nothing had been heard or seen of him for more than three days. Late one evening, Dad went out to the passage to investigate some strange noises. I saw him speaking to someone then he returned, holding by the collar an unwashed and hungry-looking Terry. It was with the greatest reluctance that he removed his jacket, as Dad had suggested, so he could have a wash. It was then that we all noticed the weals on the lad's back – it was obvious that he had been savagely beaten. Dad was so angry he wanted to call the police, but Terry would have none of that, neither would he agree that his people be informed as to his whereabouts.

It took some time to persuade him to have some supper, although it was obvious that he was ravenously hungry. While he was eating, Dad tried to question him about his beating, but Terry would not talk about it except to declare, with intense vehemence, that he was not returning home that night. He added, 'They have belted me for the last time!' Dad decided Terry should sleep with me – Terry was so grateful that he had tears in his eyes. It was a long time before Terry told me why he had been beaten. 'I was coming home from the stores with a bag of groceries when I dropped a bag of eggs and smashed the fuckin' lot!'

He was right about one thing though – he was never beaten again.

Chapter Nineteen

The hysteria of Armistice celebrations had faded, and people were now facing the stark reality of food short-ages and mass unemployment. Even able-bodied men had great difficulty in finding work, so it wasn't to be wondered at that disabled men like my father had no earthly chance.

The Christmas of 1918 was, without doubt, the worst we had ever experienced. Everything that was pawnable had gone to 'Uncle's', including most of the clothes I had been given by Irene's mother.

It was because of our desperate circumstances that Dad suffered his most humiliating experience. Without saying a word to anyone, he visited his mother and step-father to ask for help. They refused. He then called on his brother, who, being the manager of a high-class grocer, was fairly well off. He too refused.

Mother was absolutely furious. 'I would rather starve than take a crust off them,' she said.

As a last resort she visited Granddad Henderson, but he could spare very little. So, on Christmas morn-ing, Fred, young Jim and I ploughed through the snow to The Mission in Prudhoe Street, where we had our Christmas dinner, plus an apple and an orange.

But, almost overnight, there came a change in our fortunes. Dad received confirmation of the decision to admit him to the rehabilitation centre at Wallsend; he was to commence training to be a decorator on the first Monday in February 1919, and he would receive wages whilst doing so.

Even more exciting was the receipt of a letter from the Ministry of Pensions, telling him that his small pension had been increased. It also enclosed a sizeable cheque for arrears in payment.

Suddenly, everything seemed brighter. There was coal for the fire, extra grub in the pantry, most of the pawned articles had been redeemed, and most pleasing of all, Dad was beginning to look and act like the man we had known four years ago.

★ ★ ★

There were now six of us Avenue boys running about together: Bob, George, Peter, Billy, Terry and myself, and together we enjoyed taking part in any kind of mischief, although never anything malicious. We did have some scatterbrained ideas – one of which ended disastrously.

In those days, bogey-making was a favourite pastime of many boys, and we decided to make one – a large one – big enough to seat the six of us.

Our biggest problem was getting some good wheels. Most bogeys – at least in The Avenue – were equipped with wooden ones – in fact they were cut from the wooden rollers of a wringing machine. But we wanted the best.

It was Terry who provided the first pair of wheels – good ones from a pram – and he stored them in his back yard. That was on a Saturday afternoon. Two hours later, as the six of us were standing chatting, we heard some-one higher up The Avenue shouting, 'I'll kill them!' He made his way down The Avenue, screaming his blood-thirsty threats. 'What's up, hinney?' asked a nosey woman. 'What's up?' he snarled back. 'My son left his bogey outside the front door and some dirty sod has pinched the fuckin' back wheels.' He then pointed to the bogey he was pulling, 'Look at that,' he screamed.

I glanced at Terry – who was giving his fingernails an exaggerated manicure – and instantly knew who was responsible. We returned the damned wheels under cover of darkness, because the aggrieved father was about seven feet tall and built in proportion!

We eventually found what we were looking for in a scrapyard, but I was a little dubious because the wheels were about two feet in diameter. It happened that there were six of them, and some bright spark came up with the brilliant idea of making a six-wheeled bogey. Whoever heard of a six-wheeled bogey? I said it was not practicable, but I was overruled.

We nicked six lengths of flooring from an empty house, raided the axle boxes of railway wagons for grease, and then got cracking. We confined our activities to the seclusion of Billy's back yard, but when the bogey began to take shape, I expressed my doubts at the wisdom of building such a huge juggernaut. 'Oh no,' said my friends, 'The bigger the better!' (It was going to be about eight feet long and four feet wide!)

Then came the day when we gazed at the completed monster – it was as big as a bloody dray! 'Err, you know something,' said Terry, thoughtful like, 'We won't be able to get it through the fuckin' door!' He was right! We had to hoist the damn thing over the wall!

After much deliberation we decided to launch the brute on the next Sunday morning, when road traffic would be light. The venue for the test run would be Rye Hill, which was one of the first roads in Newcastle to have the cobbles removed and replaced with asphalt.

So, on a never-to be-forgotten Sunday morning, the world's first six-wheeled bogey made its initial appearance, greeted with incredulity and roars of laughter from unkind onlookers.

We received many strange looks from passers-by as we lugged the Leviathan up the hill. We ignored them, but when a passing parson solemnly made the sign of the cross we should have heeded the omen. Then a policeman, eyes gaping, approached us.

'What the hell is that?' he asked.

'A bogey.'

'You must be kidding!'

'No.'

'Are you going to ride on it?'

'Aye.'

He seemed to have difficulty controlling the muscles of his face – it was beginning to twitch! He shook his head in disbelief and turned away, giggling.

Puffing and panting, we at last reached the top of the hill, and Terry, who was the gaffer, and had decided to be the driver, took his place at the front, the steering wheel (a rope) held in his grasp.

I began to have serious misgivings as we took our places behind him, because the wheels were so huge and close together, each of us had to wrap our legs around the midriff of the lad in front.

We were ready at last, and George, who was at the rear, gave us a mighty push. The brute needed no pushing! Taken by surprise at the speed at which it shot away, George, who had only one foot on the bogey, began to find it extremely difficult getting the other one aboard.

Then came calamity number one: after hopping on that one foot at an ever-increasing speed for about twenty yards, George slipped, fell on his belly, caught his hand in the spokes of a wheel and, with an agonising yell, rolled into the gutter.

We were now going at a rare old lick and Terry yelled out, 'Put the brake on!' The so-called 'brake' was a lump of wood nailed to the side of the seat, and the idea was to scrape the end of it along the ground. Well, somebody did pull it, and it snapped! The damn bogey then came alive!

Going like the clappers, we passed a cyclist, who gave us a startled glance, and then fell off! There was no way we could use our feet because of the huge wheels, and we were all a little apprehensive as we 'whooshed' across Westmorland Road – missing a passing tram by inches.

Billy then decided he had had enough – he stood up and dived sideways over the wheels, landing on the road with a yell.

The speed of the brute was terrifying and God only knows where we would have ended up had Terry not attempted to stop it.

He inched his way forward until his feet were sticking over the front of the seat, then he thrust them hard at the ground. Well, we were going so damn fast his legs were pushed sideways and backwards and the upper part of his body simply had to go forward. Just as his face met the road, the fiendish bogey slewed sideways and we rolled over and over. I faintly heard Terry screaming in agony, 'I've split my crutch – arggh – I've split my fuckin' crutch!'

Dazed and shocked, we disentangled ourselves from the wreckage, aided by horrified onlookers. As I rose to my feet I felt a sharp pain in my right big toe. I bent down to have a look and, to my consternation, I saw a wicked-looking nail protruding through the top of my boot. Fearfully I moved my foot and the broken remains of the so-called 'brake' moved with it! Somehow, during the crash, the nail had penetrated my boot and very neatly pierced my toe. I was carried home with a lump of wood firmly attached to my foot!

Of course it had been a foolhardy escapade – as our angry parents were not slow to point out. George had lacerated fingers, Bob had sprained his ankle, Billy had to have his chin stitched and Terry walked about like a bow-legged cowboy for days afterwards because of his over-stretched crutch!

I certainly got the whole 'works' from Dad; you see, I was supposed to have been in church.

'You told a lie, you have ruined a pair of boots and your best clothes. This conduct has got to stop!' stormed Dad after I had returned from the Infirmary. But there was more.

'You will make a point of seeing the vicar, and you will tell him you wish to join St Mary's troop of Boy Scouts.'

'Scouts?' I yelled.

'Yes, Scouts!'

'But Dad—'

'No buts, you *will* join the Scouts.'

I didn't get much sympathy from Mother, 'Serve you right, you raggy-arsed young sod!'

I have to admit that I had it coming. During the whole of that summer I had been given innumerable warnings about my conduct, especially when I narrowly escaped serious injury from jumping off lorries and tramcars. But worst of all – in Dad's eyes – I had neglected my home-work, so he decided that the time had come to curb my activities.

Yet never by any stretch of imagination did I think that the punishment he imposed would take the form it did. It was too awful to contemplate. Imagine having to walk down The Avenue carrying a brush shank and wearing a cowboy hat! I would be open to every kind of ridicule – lewd or otherwise.

With a sigh of resignation I whispered, 'Baden-Powell, here I come.'

Chapter Twenty

Any lingering hopes I had that Dad would relent were soon dashed. My eleventh birthday found me enrolled in St Mary's Scouts, which I attended on Monday evenings; and choir practice meant I had to be in the church on Tuesdays and Thursdays. To complete my new code of discipline, I was allowed no more than a two-hour period of playtime on other evenings. (It pleased me a little to learn that my errant pals had suffered similar punishment!) But I do admit – quite honestly – that I never really minded my punishment; I was able, because of it, to indulge in my favourite pastime – reading. I was a young bookworm and would read any damn thing that had print on it.

I began to take a greater interest in my choir singing, a fact due in no small part to the choirmaster. Under his guidance, my voice had changed out of all recognition, so much so that I was appointed leading treble singer – and that meant singing the solo passages.

Dad had almost completed his training and hoped to find a job quickly. But despite the obvious improvement to our finances, very little could be done to improve our living conditions. It has to be said that Fred, who was nearing his fourteenth birthday, and I, now twelve, were at times acutely embarrassed by our proximity to our parents. No boy could dwell in The Avenue without being made fully aware of the facts of life at an early age. Fred and I were no exception.

Dad undoubtedly realised the awkwardness of the situation, but in fairness, there was little or nothing he could do about it. Fred was suffering more than anyone; the dark, damp box-room in which we slept was the chief cause of the worsening of his chest condition – and he was never afraid to voice his objections openly and frequently. However, his life was to become very much brighter thanks to the kind action of a lady who was then the caretaker of a Jewish boys' school in Rye Hill. Before conversion, it had been a large detached house and two or three bedrooms had remained unaltered. That lady had already befriended Fred's pal Jack, and had provided him with a bed in one of those rooms.

Imagine Fred's delight when she invited him to share the room with his pal. I was equally delighted. At least he would be sleeping in warm, airy surroundings – it was in fact literally what the doctors had ordered. But my parents were a little reluctant at first. I suppose the fact that Fred would be sleeping away from home made them feel guilty. However, his health had been so worrying that it would have been daft – indeed criminal – to deny him the conditions he so urgently needed.

Because of the extra money Dad was earning, Christmas 1919 was quite a cheerful affair. There were small presents for us, but the thing we enjoyed most was having the seasonal dinner in our own house.

I mentioned in a previous chapter how lucky I was as far as my health was concerned. That was true, of course, and I was grateful for it – at least my parents didn't have any worries on that score. But I was extremely lucky in other ways; for instance I was still the best-dressed boy in The Avenue, thanks to gifts of clothing I received from two good people.

Irene's mother gave me another lot of clothes – some of them fitted Fred, which was especially pleasing. The second gift was made as a result of tragedy. One of the singers in the choir – a Mr Slater – suffered a dreadful bereavement when his son overbalanced while sliding down some banisters and was killed. The following week he brought a parcel of suits that had belonged to the dead boy and asked me to accept them. Gifts like that were a boon because keeping us decently dressed was one of Mother's biggest headaches. At least it meant I would have enough clothing to last me the rest of that year.

Oh yes, the Scouts! I had almost forgotten!

Mother had made an intensive search of all the second-hand shops and had come up with a battered old hat and a khaki blouse. (Dad had promised to buy me some new ones later.) I was sorely troubled, not so much at the thought of joining the troop, but at the greeting I could expect in The Avenue when I made my first appearance dressed in Scout's uniform.

When I returned home after my initiation (I was not in uniform) there was much sniggering when I imparted the information that I was a member of the 'Peewit patrol'. 'Some Peewit,' said my sarcastic brother.

By now the time had come to expose myself in uniform. Filled with trepidation, I looked through the kitchen window hoping to see an empty Avenue, but alas, the blooming street was crowded.

'Off you go,' said Dad.

'On your way,' said Mother.

'Ah, is the little Peewit afraid?' (That was Fred!)

The fact that Dad came to the front door when I left didn't have any effect on Thug and his cohorts, because as soon as I appeared there was an immediate cacophony, which continued until I turned the corner of a side street. I almost wept!

But there was a sequel to those outrageous cat-calls. I wasn't aware that my now firm friend Terry had been an interested onlooker and that he had intervened in the only way he knew – by thumping some of Thug's pals!

His invitation to Thug to 'have a go' was declined. Terry, of course, had an old score to settle with that brute – as had I – but whereas I had been forbidden to indulge in street fighting, he was not restricted in any way. There was the fact that my pal, then fourteen years old, had become a stocky and dangerous individual to tangle with, something that all concerned were beginning to realise.

Perhaps I should have retaliated on my own behalf against the constant sneers and jibes from that unholy mob of ruffians, despite Dad's warning, but I knew perfectly well I was not equipped to deal with the ferocity which was the stock-in-trade of those vicious hooligans.

You know, Dad often described me as being 'accident prone'. Well, damn me if I didn't confirm that dubious description after only four weeks as a Scout.

Physical training played an integral part in Scouting activities – it still does I think – and our leader's favourite exercise was for us to perform – Tarzan-like – on a rope suspended from the ceiling. Each boy would stand on a wooden horse at one end of the room. The idea was to swing from the horse and land on a thick mat at the other end of the room. Simple! Of course it was!

I mounted the horse and stood alongside one of the older Scouts, who, when I had grasped the rope, gave me a terrific push. Like a man on a flying trapeze I flew through the air – then the bloody rope freed itself from the ceiling! I continued flying, and my momentum was such that I zipped over the mat, through an open door and landed face first in the passage beyond. The upshot of all that was finding myself, for the third time in my young life, sitting in the Infirmary, this time to have my badly split upper lip stitched.

'What in the world are we going to do with you?' sighed Dad.

Chapter Twenty-One

The year 1920 was, so far, proving to be the best of the four and a half we had spent in The Avenue. Dad had obtained employment as a painter and he had been assured that prospects were very good. He once again made an attempt to obtain a better house, but it was the same old story, there wasn't any to be had.

Naturally, he was angry and very, very bitter. 'This,' he said, 'is the country I fought for, that millions of men died for, the country "fit for heroes to live in", and they cannot even provide me with a decent house.'

I noticed that he was drinking again, not heavily perhaps, but regularly, and because of it those abominable rows between him and Mother resumed. And it was one of those argie-bargies that was to culminate in a rib-tickling finale midway through that year.

It began on a Saturday afternoon, when Dad, contrary to his normal practice of returning home from work and then going to the local for a pint, decided to have a couple on the way home. I could appreciate Mother's concern at his lateness but when he eventually arrived home, singing quietly to himself, she did quite the wrong thing by lambasting him for coming home late – after all, he hadn't done it before. Normally, Dad was a cheerful soul whilst under the influence and he usually dealt with her outbursts in a good-tempered manner – but not on that particular day. There developed, within minutes, the most almighty slanging match I had ever witnessed between them. In fact, Dad was so incensed by some particularly harsh comment, he did something that was completely out of character; he tried to hit her. Perhaps Mother realised that she had gone too far, or perhaps she was afraid, because she donned her coat and walked out. Dad said nothing and after a while he decided to have a sleep in my bed. (That was the usual weekend procedure.)

Come tea time no Mother! Come supper time, she was still missing, but Dad didn't appear perturbed in any way.

In the meantime I had located Fred, who simply said, 'This had to happen sooner or later.' Our kitchen was strangely quiet that evening. Dad just sat, saying little, and when he packed me and the two young ones off to bed, I began to feel anxious and afraid.

The smell of breakfast being cooked the next morning got us out of bed, but there was still no sign of Mother.

As the time approached for me to toddle off to church, I asked Dad if I should skip it to help look after young Jim and Dora. 'No,' he replied, 'you go along.'

I hurried home after the service and found to my dismay that there was still no sign of Mother. In reply to my anxious question, he half smiled and said, 'It's alright son, I know where she is.'

While I had been away he had cooked the meat and peeled the spuds, and as it was then close to twelve o'clock, he decided to nip out for half an hour. He was as good as his word – after having a couple of pints he looked, indeed *was*, in a much more cheerful frame of mind.

The climax to this story began as he was about to put the spuds on to boil.

The door opened, we both turned around, and there stood Mother! Dad looked at her and, without any change of expression, grabbed a tattie from the pan and shied it at her. She ducked to avoid the missile then Dad heaved another one, then another and another, and he would have contin-

ued but my scandalised Mother decided to make a hasty exit.
I was somewhat dumbfounded by Dad's behaviour, but I was
absolutely amazed to see him shaking with inward laughter!

He stood, listening to Mother talking to someone on
the landing, and he still had another spud in his hand.
Suddenly the door was opened very quickly. When
a figure appeared Dad swiftly threw that spud – and it
smacked Grandfather Henderson right in his ginger tash!
The startled man jumped back, hand over his mouth,
then with an inarticulate yell of rage, he bent down,
picked up a couple of those tubers and threw them at
Dad, whose turn it became to take evasive action.

Suddenly he held up his hands in mock surren-
der and burst into roars of laughter, but my aggrieved
Grandfather took some little time to simmer down. It
was only the tears of young Jim and Dora that brought
the outrageous scene to an end.

When my parents and Grandfather sat down to talk
I was told to 'take a walk'. I never did learn what followed – but the events of those twenty-four hours left
me depressed and miserable; a condition, I am sure, that
did not go unnoticed by my parents.

I was at an impressionable age – nearly twelve – and
during the five years of living in The Avenue, I had witnessed, with disgust, the rows and obscene arguments
indulged in by other families. 'Damn it all,' I thought,
'We are no better!' Of course, the cramped conditions of
this infested tenement was not conducive to permanent
peace, so I suppose allowances had to be made when
sheer frustration was the usual cause of disharmony.

But as I said, I never was to learn what transpired
between my parents and my Grandfather, but there was
never to be another scene comparable to that of the spud
throwing incident. They must have realised that any further deterioration in family life would prove disastrous
– especially to us kids.

★ ★ ★

The year 1920 was notable for many things, including the fact that Fred and Terry would soon be leaving school. Incidentally, Fred had made a tremendous effort to make up the schooling he had lost whilst in hospital, and though he had done magnificently, his headteacher informed Dad that his stammer would be a great handicap. Sympathy was wasted on Fred, because he had decided to seek open-air employment.

I was living what could only be termed a 'full life' during that period. There was choir practice twice a week and I was singing in church twice each Sunday. (Which reminds me, I sang my first solo in church on Easter Sunday of that year, and in the congregation were Dad and Mother, and Irene and her mother. Quite an occasion!)

Dad, however, was proving to be a real martinet as far as my homework was concerned, and I began to wonder not only what he had in mind for me, but for how much longer I had to keep my nose to the grindstone.

There was only one way to find out – I asked him. 'You have been running about like a damned lunatic far too long. I am determined to make you study hard because I do not want you to make the same mistake I made.'

That period was particularly notable for the terrible increase in the number of deaths from TB. Fred was very vulnerable during that awful period and he was a source of great anxiety to our parents. They therefore decided that he should continue to take advantage of Mrs Matlock's kindness and sleep at her home as often as circumstances would allow. As for me, well, I was a healthy young bugger, wasn't I? It was remarkable though that I never suffered of any kind, not even a cold, during the years I lived in The Avenue.

I often wondered how the hell any of us survived at all. For instance, there was the day that the six of us decided to go to Jesmond Dene for a swim. We usually frequented the public baths, but that particular day was scorching hot, much too hot to trudge to Jesmond even, so we made our minds up to have a swim in the Tyne.

'I know of a good spot,' said Terry.

'Where?' we chorused.

'It's not far from here and there is a canny little diving board.'

We allowed ourselves to be persuaded and made our way to his canny little spot. It was at the bottom of Forth Banks!

We stood on the jetty-cum-diving board, gazing with acute distaste at the oily water flowing past, but Terry wasted no time. He flung off his clothes and dived in, starkers! The rest of us stood and watched him cavorting in the water. 'Howwaay, it's lovely,' he yelled. So five foolish lads dived in after him.

We had been in just a few minutes when I heard Bobby yelling. I swam towards him and he pointed. 'Look at that!' 'That' was a huge salmon, but long dead, and it was floating towards us with it's sightless fish-eyes fixed balefully on us. Just as it passed us I heard Billy screaming blue murder. We paddled towards him and reached him at the moment a brown object latched onto his lug-hole. He swiped it off (it was a big brown turd!) and shouted, 'Look over there!' We looked, and what we saw made us sick, we were swimming I under a six-foot open sewer.

Holding our breaths we scrambled to the bank and went searching for Muckian. We were too late; he was halfway up Forth Banks!

How did any of us survive after pranks like that?

Of the many incidents of 1920, the one that stands out most in my memory had its origin at home.

It began on a Sunday evening, when Dad and Fred were discussing the kind of job most suitable for Fred and I was engrossed in the capers of a ghost in *Comic Cuts*.

'Dad, have you ever seen a ghost?' I asked, jokingly. To my astonishment he almost went down my throat.

'What the devil has made you ask that?'

I just shrugged my shoulders and carried on reading. But I noticed that Fred was looking at Dad in an odd manner, in fact I am sure he was about to ask him a question when Dad sighed and said, 'Sorry I snapped, but now you have asked, the answer is yes.'

Mother interrupted, 'Do you think you should?' I just stared in disbelief but Fred had a kind of 'I knew it' look on his face.

'Yes,' replied Dad, 'they are old enough now, and it will clear up those mysteries of years ago.'

It was when he said 'those mysteries' that I began to understand Fred's knowing look; had he not said repeatedly that something bad had happened when we lived in Gill Street?

We waited in silence for him to begin, and I can assure you that the tale he unfolded could have come straight from the pen of Edgar Allan Poe. Judge for yourselves, read the ghostly narrative as it was told to us, in his own words.

My Father's Ghost Story

I am sure you will both remember that at one time I was employed at a local colliery which was situated about three miles from Benwell, where we used to live in Gill Street. I was a deputy and shot-firer and I usually worked alternative fortnights of the day- and nightshifts.

At the time this story begins, extensive re-organisation was being carried out in various districts underground, and as a consequence I was ordered a period of twelve-hour day-shifts, with a starting time of 4 a.m.

I normally cycled to and from the pit but the day before I was due to start the first of the long shifts, I discovered that the front wheel was buckled. So, not only did it mean I would have to walk, but it also meant I would have to leave home much earlier – somewhere about 2.45 a.m.

The route to the colliery was by way of unlit country lanes, which, though quite pleasant to walk along in daylight, could be most depressing during the hours of darkness, especially if the weather was bad.

However, I was aware that a number of local lads who were employed at the colliery walked there every morning when on the early shift, so I agreed to meet them at Benwell parish church at 2.30 a.m. After all, there is nothing better than cheerful company on a long, dreary walk.

There were no problems on the first three days of that week, but things went a little awry on the Thursday.

As I normally did, I wound my watch up the night before and checked that the alarm clock was set for 1.45. I rose when the alarm sounded, then washed, dressed, packed a sandwich and filled my bottle with tea.

I was about to sit down and enjoy a cup of tea and a cigarette when I happened to glance at the watch and, to my consternation, it showed the time to be 2.45!

I tiptoed into my bedroom and checked the alarm clock, which showed the same time. Now that puzzled me a little because I had always kept the clock at least fifteen minutes fast. But I had no time to ponder over it because I was close to being a half-hour late, and my companions would be well on their way.

My main worry was missing the riding times, which are periods at the beginning and end of shifts, when men are raised and lowered. When all the men have been dealt with, the cages resume the business of coal drawing and will normally continue to do so whilst it is available. Therefore, late-comers have to wait until there is a break in the coal drawing, and that could mean a wait of anything up to two hours.

I set off at a brisk pace, knowing that I could still make it to the pit in time – providing I didn't fall and break my toe or something.

Of course it would have to be a dark and foggy morning – I couldn't even see the church clock – and after I had stumbled a few times hurrying along Benwell Lane, I simply had to slow down.

To add to my discomfort icy rain began to fall, and soon my only guide was the silhouette of the hedgerows.

I wasn't sure how long I had been walking, but suddenly I passed through what could be described as a patch of frozen mist and with a shiver I turned up the collar of my coat.

I continued on my way and after going a short distance I was surprised, but very relieved, to have left the icy patch behind. But for some unaccountable reason I began to feel uneasy, and silly though it may sound, I had an instinctive feeling that I was not alone – that someone or something was looking at me!

Feeling a little self-conscious, I looked to my right and left and then behind me, but I could see nothing, not even a sheep or a cow.

I realised then that my nerves were getting a little jumpy, so I gave myself a stern lecture and continued on my way. But after just a few yards I stopped in my tracks, because from the corner of my eye I had seen some movement.

I looked to the right and as I focussed my eyes on a gap in the hedge, I saw a figure appear, and it had materialised from nothing!

It was of a stygian blackness and stood out in plain relief against the folds of the fog. Dressed in what resembled a monk's habit, it stood motionless, and I began to tremble with fear.

Time stood still and my mind was in a whirl as I stood and gazed at the thing, then, in a shaking voice, I called out, 'Hey, who the hell are you?' But the thing didn't respond.

I was debating what I ought to do when I heard the faint sound of men's voices – and never was a sound more welcome!

With a sigh of relief, I turned to face the owners of the voices and as I did the apparition appeared to zoom away at lightening speed. I walked to the gap in the hedge but there was nothing to see and I began to wonder if my eyes had been playing tricks. Well, maybe they had, but when the men appeared I must confess I was badly shaken.

But I was in for another surprise, because the men turned to be those with whom I had walked the three previous three mornings! They stopped when they saw me and when I walked towards them one of them said, 'You must have been in a hurry this morning.' I pulled out my watch and, by the flickering light of a match, I saw the time to be 3.10. 'Oh no,' I replied, 'You lot are late.' They consulted their watches and proved that mine was twenty minutes fast!

I made no further comment as I moved off with them. But inwardly I was troubled. What bothered me most was how my watch had come to gain twenty minutes over-night; it was a good watch and had always been a most reliable time-keeper, so what had gone wrong with it?

The only answer I could think of was that I had inad-vertently moved the pointers when winding it up. But that particular watch needed a key to both wind it up and adjust the pointers. The more I thought about it the more confused I became, so I decided to try and forget the whole incident.

I gave only an occasional thought to it during the long shift underground, and when I returned to the surface I laughed at myself – I *must* have been seeing things!

I didn't mention the experiences to your mother; she would have said I was barmy, but you can well imagine my feelings when I checked the alarm clock and found it was twenty minutes fast! What had been more disturbing was to find the watch showing exactly the same time as the church clock! So what in heaven's name had hap-pened? I came to the conclusion that I had misread the time on both watch and clock, so the best thing for me to do was to forget the whole thing.

I hadn't a great deal of time to think about the incident; foremost in my activities was a request for an interview with the management. Having made up my mind to have a go at the management side of mining, I wanted to ascertain what the prospects were. Well, I had the interview and it proved to be a waste of time, even though they were very sympathetic and appreciated my desire to further my career. As one of the board had said, 'You know how it is here, promotion has to be based on seniority, and even then someone has to retire or die before a vacancy is created.'

The thought of having to wait for some unfortunate official to die didn't go down too well with me – neither did the prospect of getting into a rut. I came to a decision as I pedalled home after the interview – I would try my luck at another colliery.

One in particular came to mind where prospects would be reasonably good, and that was a pit at which your mother's two uncles worked. To put the record straight, those two gentlemen were married to your mother's aunts.

I wasted no time in contacting your Grandfather Henderson – the two ladies were his sisters – and he readily agreed to find out what the prospects were of obtaining employment at that pit.

But when I informed your mother of my intentions, she flatly refused to even consider moving, and consequently we had a terrific row and tempers were frayed for weeks.

However, during the second week of November, I received the news that there were vacancies and I needed only to make a formal application, so, despite your mother's objections, I applied and was successful.

There was one snag though – a colliery house could not be provided for at least a month and that would have meant moving at Christmas, which would have been too upsetting. But the management generously agreed to hold the vacancy for me until the January of 1914, not that it made any difference to your mother — she was dead against it.

In the meantime, I had been ordered to do a further spell of twelve-hour shifts, but fortunately I had repaired my bike and that meant I need not leave home until 3.30 a.m.

I was feeling a little depressed on that Monday morning when I set off; I was in fact brooding about the uncertainty of my future. What was more — and I find it difficult to explain — I had an inexplicable feeling of fear, but of what I was not able to fathom.

As befits November, it was a very dark and frosty morning and so slippery was the rough road off Benwell Lane that I had to take very great care.

I had travelled about five hundred yards along the lane when suddenly, by the feeble light of my lamp, I saw a man appear in front of me. I shouted and veered sharply to my left, losing my balance as I did so.

I quickly picked myself up and watched angrily as the 'man' glided through the air towards the fence.

I stood motionless, looking at the man, who now stood at the exact spot that the other THING had occupied!

Shivering, and yet with my body bathed in sweat, I stood transfixed, just gazing at the thing. It stood out clearly and, like the other apparition, it was dressed in a long robe, but in addition it was wearing a long pointed cap.

I remained rooted to the spot and began to babble incoherently when it lifted an arm, until it was pointed over my head.

It was the movement of the arm that convinced me I was looking at something supernatural, and, though I have never considered myself to be a coward, I was, at that moment, shaking with pure terror, and for the first time in many, many years, I began to pray.

For what seemed an eternity I stood motionless, and I could sense an aura of evilness emanating from the accursed thing. Then from somewhere I found enough strength to yell and at the same time I flung my bike at it. I watched fearfully when it suddenly zoomed away from me at an incredible speed, getting smaller and smaller until it disappeared into the darkness beyond.

Sorely troubled, I mounted the bike and set off to return home, but then I asked myself if that was the wise thing to do – after all, I could hardly rouse your mother and tell her I had seen a ghost!

With a sigh I turned and continued my journey to the pit, and when I arrived there I hurriedly drew my lamp and made my way immediately to the pit-head platform – I was in no mood to listen to idle chatter from my mates.

As you know – at least I have told you often enough – mining is a dangerous occupation and it demands from all those employed in it extreme care, alertness and concentration, and that applies even more so when blasting is taking place.

After such an unnerving experience I wondered how I was going to cope, but so hard had I to concentrate on the placing of charges that the memory of that unpleasant encounter began to recede, and after I had placed and fired the first blasting I felt decidedly better.

My next job was in another district and as I slowly made my way there I had almost forgotten about the damned shadow.

I had reached the junction of the main hauling road when I noticed a long line of lights coming towards me, and my first thoughts were that maybe there had been a heavy fall of stone somewhere.

I recognised the leading figure as a deputy-overman, but before I could ask what was wrong he said, 'Make your way out, Sam, there's been an accident.' I knew then that it had been a fatal one.

Under normal circumstances I would have been sorry, but not unduly upset by such news, but to learn of it so soon after the traumatic experience of a few hours earlier proved too much for me – I almost ran to the shaft bottom!

When I reached the surface I learned that an overman had been killed and two men seriously injured in a massive fall of stone.

The full impact of what had happened, or it's implications, didn't strike me until I had travelled almost halfway home, when the words of the management at my interview came to mind; 'Someone has to move up, retire or die.'

I jumped off the bike. Dear God, I thought, an overman has just died and there is now a vacancy!

Odd thoughts began running through my mind. Was that man's death in any conceivable way connected with that apparition? Had that 'thing' by some unnatural power contrived to have the poor man killed? Was I to gain promotion by stepping into that unfortunate man's shoes?

My head was spinning as I remounted my bike and continued the journey home, and of one thing I was sure – I simply had to talk to someone, and as I neared the parish church I thought, who better than the vicar?

I entered the church but unfortunately the vicar was not in attendance so I left a message asking him to call to the house.

I remember seeing you two when I entered the scullery, but I was too disturbed to bother with you.

I took your mother into the bedroom and told her everything. I described in detail my two encounters with what I firmly believed had been ghosts, and quite naturally she was disturbed because she well knew I was not an imaginative type of man.

I washed and dressed then hurried off to Ashington where the colliery was situated. The outcome was that I would begin my new job three weeks later – I certainly had no intention of returning to the present one.

When I returned home I found the vicar waiting, and to him I unburdened my troubled mind, after which I felt a little more composed.

You were right, Fred, the dead man was the father of the two boys for whom your school said a prayer. So there it is; now you know the reason for the letter I gave you to hand to the Headmaster, which informed him we were moving to Ashington.

Just a final word. Over the years since it happened, I have almost convinced myself that my own eyes may have deceived me, but I can think of no logical reason why my watch should gain twenty minutes and then right itself.

★ ★ ★

From the manner in which Dad had told us that story, it was obvious that he had been badly affected by the incident, and it was never referred to again. But of one thing I am sure – the trials and tribulations which were to befall my family began on that Monday morning on Benwell Lane in the month of November 1913.

Chapter Twenty-Two

I suppose all communities have their share of odd-ball characters, and The Avenue was no exception. For instance, above us lived a drunk and his alcoholic wife. But I doubt if any area could have boasted a more complete tomboy than our 'Battling Fanny'! Actually her real name was Mary, but woe betides any misguided individual who addressed her thus. Biologically, of course, she was a female, but in every other aspect she looked and acted like a male. (The local barber wouldn't bat an eyelid when she asked for a 'short back and sides'!)

Her voice was deep and gravelly; she always dressed in male attire, and she had a physique that was the envy of many lads her age. Her boxing ability was well known and feared, and she could out-run, out-jump and out-swear most of her male counterparts. But she cursed the fact that she was well endowed 'titty-wise' and freely admitted they were a 'friggin' nuisance!' She even wrapped bandages around them to make them inconspicuous. Most of us liked her, but oh boy did she like a game of football!

I first witnessed her versatility while the gang was having a kick-around in the park. We had just split into two teams when she rolled up. 'I will be the goalkeeper,' she announced, and not one of us dared show dissent.

In order to balance the sides, Terry approached some youths who were standing nearby and asked one of them to join us – he agreed. I noticed that Terry was talking earnestly to him, then the stranger laughed and nodded his head.

With a lopsided grin on his face, my pal said to me, 'You will see some fun shortly!'

'What do you mean?' I asked. He laughed, 'Just watch!'

I didn't know what he was talking about, but the so-called fun began after just a few minutes when the stranger barged into Fanny and dumped her on her bum. She picked herself up, walked up to the offender and, in a menacing voice, said, 'Do that again and I will knock your fuckin' block off!' But the youth made a derisive gesture and walked away.

I noticed that Terry was grinning broadly and I asked him what was so funny. 'I asked the lad to give the goal-keeper a good thumping,' he replied. 'What's so funny about that?' I asked. 'He doesn't know she's Battling Fanny!' he chortled.

I was very little the wiser, but the 'fun' my friend had been laughing about was soon to begin. In fact, it began immediately after she had been sent sprawling once again by the new lad.

She picked herself up and walked to the railings that encircled the park, where she removed her sweater and then the long bandage that was wrapped around her chest. She carefully hung them on the railings then turned and walked towards the lad who had flattened her twice.

'Turn around you,' she growled. The lad turned and for the life of me I couldn't describe the expression that came over his face. There was bewilderment, awe, shock, lust maybe, or perhaps a combination of all four, because what met his eyes was a semi-naked young woman standing a few feet away from him.

Her fists were raised and only partially concealing a pair of luscious watermelons. She did a couple of nifty sidesteps and those bouncing orbs gyrated in a wildly titillating manner. There was no doubt about it, he was mesmerised by those dancing tits!

He watched, eyes bulging and mouth agape as she drew nearer, but the shock of seeing an exposed pair of wallopers had proved too much for him, he was transfixed! Suddenly Fanny swung a lightening fast right hook and belted him on the lug-hole, and the obvious pain brought him out of his trance – well, sort of! The befuddled lad rolled his eyes, emitted an hysterical giggle and then bolted as though the Devil himself was after him!

We all fell about laughing, but couldn't help feeling sorry for the poor sod – how was he going to explain his thick ear?

There comes to mind another queer character, and queer is the operative word!

The person in question answered to the name of 'Little Jesus' (I offer my humble apologies to The Lord!) He was a short man, about five feet in height, but he was, in fact, the most corrupt man I have ever met. When he first arrived in The Avenue with his spouse, there were no children, but after eight years there were eight of them – one for each year! One would have thought that after such a prolific output his sexual appetite would have been sated, but no, not the dirty little bugger – he had a sideline.

His part-time occupation was brought to light when a parson was arrested in the Haymarket for importuning males. Complete with dog collar he was marched off to the 'nick', where interrogation revealed the 'priest' to be none other than our short-arsed neighbour. He eventually appeared before the magistrates and was extremely lucky to be bound over. But now you know why he was nicknamed Little Jesus!

I well remember an encounter Terry and I had with him. We were standing in a narrow lane that skirted the rear of The Avenue when Terry said, 'Blimey, here comes the puff!' Because there wasn't much room and neither of us wanted to make contact with him, we stood close to the wall with our backs to him.

He didn't look at us, but as he was passing he dropped one of his hands and gently caressed Terry's arse. Like an outraged maiden, my pal jumped about three feet into the air and yelled, 'Did you see that, eh, did you see what he did?' I tried hard not to laugh.

Terry wasn't having that! 'Hey you, Little Jesus, come here!'

'Yes darling?' Little Jesus squeaked.

He squealed like a little girl when a boot was planted on his posterior. 'Oops, darling, that hurts!' he shrilled, trying to protect his arse and at the same time shouting, 'Ooh! Aah! Ooh! Aah!'

Little Jesus was to continue as a pint-sized stud with unabated ardour – four more little children joined his herd during the following four years!

Chapter Twenty-Three

The year 1920 kept bowling along with little of any real interest taking place. Dad was still working regularly and Fred, much to his delight, had obtained employment in a shipyard.

There was one incident though that culminated in Dad almost being sent to prison.

The events leading up to it began in our kitchen one morning at about 4 a.m., when Dad and Mother were roused from their sleep by the hysterical cries of young Dora. When Dad investigated, he was horrified to find scores of cockroaches in the kids' bed – she was being almost eaten alive by the filthy things. So outraged was he that he took a day off work and went storming into the Town Hall.

On being told there was little hope of any kind of action, he went berserk. He stormed from office to office looking for someone in authority, and eventually the police were called when he confronted the Lord Mayor and told him a few home truths.

Well, Dad had asked for trouble, because no matter how justified the grievance may be, to threaten the number one citizen was a heinous crime!

Fortunately the charges against Dad were dropped – no doubt the possible publicising of the dreadful conditions in which people were living played a major part in that decision.

My own life was continuing as Dad had decided – Scouts, choir and homework.

There was one dark cloud hanging over me though; in a few more weeks I would be leaving St Nick's and, having spent more than six years in that cosy little school with kind teachers, I viewed with some misgiving the transfer to a larger establishment.

I must admit that Dad's insistence that I 'knuckle down to it' had proved beneficial.

I was well aware that I possessed an active brain – a fact that was borne out by my excellent school reports – but I cannot deny that my good progress was due in no small way to Dad's heavy hand.

It came to me gradually what it was he had in mind for me. You see, he had often talked to Fred and I about his early days, of his father and grandfather and how he himself had decided to forego higher education. 'That,' he would say emphatically, 'was my biggest mistake.'

I suppose the increased pressure he put on me stemmed from his keen disappointment that Fred could not have benefited from further education. He had the ability, but he also had a very bad chest complaint, and his stammer, if anything, had worsened.

But I, a healthy young bugger with a fair amount of intelligence should have little trouble in getting the most out of my schooling. So Dad said.

★ ★ ★

Shortly before my twelfth birthday, I once again brushed with my old enemy, Thug. I had almost completely ignored him for two or three years, and I suppose it was my disdainful attitude that began to infuriate him – he had to have a go at me somehow. But the way in which he did it, and the occasion he chose to carry it out, not only sickened me, but embarrassed the good people I was with.

It happened on the morning when our newly built parish hall was to be opened and blessed by the Dean of St Nicholas' Cathedral. The new hall was sited at the bottom of Rye Hill, and after much discussion it had been decided that the dignitaries from the cathedrals should be led by the choir, in a procession from St Mary's Church to the new hall.

The impending opening and procession had become common knowledge throughout the area, and as I made my way to the church to prepare, I could see that quite a good crowd were already lining the pavement on Rye Hill.

The walk began with the choir lustily singing 'Onward Christian Soldiers' and everything was going smoothly – until we reached the junction of Cambridge Street, when, to my horror Thug and his cronies ranged up alongside me.

There was little anyone could have done about it; that evil youth respected no one and cared little what people thought. I suppose it could have been deemed comical when he began to sing in unison with the choir, but the words he was using were obscene and couldn't be heard by the onlookers.

His scandalous behaviour proved too much for one of the bass singers, who gave him a sharp push and sent him sprawling. Thug picked himself up and with a venomous look on his face he came for me, and, in trying to avoid him, I stumbled and sent two other choirboys sprawling.

Some of the onlookers were yelling at Thug, but he simply answered with derisive gestures. I was speechless with rage and when I recovered my balance I impulsively went after him, but a man moved swiftly from the crowd and grabbed me by the shoulders. 'No you don't,' said Dad, 'Get back to your place.'

He was right of course; that was neither the time nor the place for retaliation. In any case, he was still too good for me!

There was a sequel to that unpleasant incident, about which I knew nothing until after the ceremony. The accompanying policeman had been quick to spot the trouble and had apprehended Thug. He administered his own brand of summary punishment – a couple of old-fashioned clips around the lug-hole! In so doing he added fuel to the burning hatred that Thug had for me. Oh yes, I had to prepare myself for the day when avoidance of my enemy's determination to 'get me' would be impossible.

With not a little regret we turned and looked at St Nick's for the last time; how incredibly fast six years seemed to have passed. Contrary to our normal animated chatter we were very subdued as we wended our way along Forth Street.

Irene appeared to be particularly affected by the fact that we were walking home together for the last time – at least from school – and to be honest I too was filled with a sense of great sadness.

You may think we were much too young to indulge in such strong sentimentality, but remember, for almost six years we had walked to and from school every day and I had been a frequent visitor to her home. Was it so surprising then that we had a great affection for each other?

I had been informed that my next school would be Cambridge Street, and I had hoped that Irene too would be able to attend there, but her mother had made different plans for her – she was to be a pupil at Rutherford Girls' College. However, I knew I would often see her in church on Sundays.

But quite a few interesting – and amusing – incidents were to occur in The Avenue before that year ended, and let us begin with Terry, shall we?

He had left school and become apprenticed to – of all people – a Jewish master painter! However, after having worked for a couple of months, he considered himself grown up, and decided to act like one.

He therefore nipped into an off-license one Saturday evening and bought himself a couple of bottles of strong beer – which he consumed with great gusto in the grounds of the parish church.

So exhilarated did he feel that he bought another couple and repeated the procedure. About an hour later he was rolling all over the place, singing his damned head off. (He told me later he had slept it off in somebody's back garden!)

It would be after eleven o'clock when he made his way home – to find the front door locked. (It transpired that his family had learned of his drunken escapade and locked him out.)

He wasn't unduly worried because he knew there was free sleeping accommodation nearby – under the wringer behind our front door! So he crept noiselessly into our passage and crawled under the mangle, where he curled himself up on the iron bearer. So far so good.

Still feeling the effects of the beer he soon dozed off, but he was suddenly brought back to full consciousness by the sound of the front door being opened. With bated breath he watched as two figures tiptoed in, and closing the door very quietly, they then took up position in the front of the wringer.

At this point I should mention that in the rear tenement above us lived a widow, two sons and a daughter, whose name was Nancy. She was about nineteen years old and worked in a city florist. She was a nice girl (too old for me!) but her aspirations were similar to mine – she wanted away from The Avenue.

She was being courted by someone who lived in a much more respectable area, and just occasionally he would escort her to the front door and then depart rather hastily (The Avenue was no place for strangers during the hours of darkness).

On this particular night though he must have thrown discretion to the wind – or maybe they both felt in

an amorous mood – because almost immediately they
began canoodling in a rather passionate manner. And
under the wringer was Terry!

His nose was only a few inches from Nancy's legs,
and with his mouth wide open and his eyes bulging he
crouched there hardly daring to breathe. However, after
some ardent osculation and determined groping by her
boyfriend, Nancy must have realised that the situation
was getting out of hand because she suddenly hissed
'Stop it!' But he ignored her and continued his activities
with increasing fervour.

By then Terry had stuffed his hankie into his mouth to
stifle his laughter but the situation became more hilarious when his startled eyes beheld Nancy's knickers being
pulled down and up, down and up!

It proved too much for him and from his throat came
a kind of muted gurgle. 'What's that?' squeaked lover
boy, but Nancy took advantage of the lull in the passion
battle and hot-footed it up the stairs. Romeo, however,
had passed the point of no return and raced after her to
the upper landing, where further scuffling took place.

Terry was then almost bursting with suppressed laughter, and on impulse poked his head out from under the
wringer and shouted, 'For Christ's sake get them off and
let a man get some sleep!' Silence suddenly prevailed,
then Nancy uttered a horrified 'Eeek' and the shocked
boy almost jumped the whole flight of stairs in one go
before galloping up The Avenue and into the night.

There was an interested onlooker during the later part of
the comedy – your humble! Remember the small window
above my head? Well, it had been left open, as usual, and I
heard the sound of the lovers quite plainly. I had become
accustomed to the various noises of tenants walking up
and down the stairs, but I hadn't listened to such a com-
motion as that before – so I decided to close the window.

It was only curiosity that prompted me to have a peep
before I closed it, and as I gazed at the two figures one

of them broke away and ran upstairs. It was then that I heard that damned rat-bag Terry holler out to them.

He told me all about it later and also made an observation of the kind that only he could think up. 'I wonder what would have happened if I had grabbed that bloke's hand?' he said, with his usual dirty laugh.

I doubt whether Nancy ever discovered the identity of the voyeur – albeit an unwilling one. Certainly neither Terry nor I ever talked about it to anyone.

Chapter Twenty-Four

It was Dad who set me thinking during the festive season of 1920/21, when he suddenly said to me, 'I don't want you to become too involved in the church.'

I just looked at him as he continued, 'You are attending four times every week, and now you are considering spending more time in the place.'

He was referring to my decision to take lessons in scripture with the object of being confirmed.

Truth to tell, I wasn't too sure what my feelings were towards church; I really enjoyed singing with the choir, but that wasn't actually worship, was it?

It is worth mentioning that religion played a very, very small part in the lives of The Avenue inhabitants. Apart from the Catholics, who attended church mainly through fear, very few of them, young or old, attended any kind of chapel, and, honestly speaking, no one could blame them, because their lives were dominated by filth, vermin and starvation – the sort of abominations for which religion was not the cure. In fact, their oft repeated reply to any misguided parson trying to increase his fold was, 'A spiritual lecture doesn't kill beetles or fill an empty belly!'

But I remembered the smug look on Dad's face when he read my St Nick's school report, as if to say, 'I knew you could do it!'

I had to agree that his insistence on my working harder at school was now fully justified, and I looked forward to my new school with eagerness and confidence.

And so, on a cold January morning, I stood in the corridor of Cambridge Street School – and I didn't like what I saw. This place was the very antithesis of St Nick's.

Gone was the warm, friendly atmosphere; in its place there was a clinical coldness that was almost chilling.

I had become accustomed to the sound of happy voices and joyous laughter, but as I watched the pupils march, silent and unsmiling, from the Assembly Hall to their classrooms, I became extremely depressed. And the appearance of teachers garbed in gowns and mortar-boards did little to alleviate my apprehension.

Accompanied by Mother, I had been interviewed the previous day by the Headmaster, and, in order to assess my ability, I had undergone a written test, and that is why I was standing in the corner awaiting his pleasure.

The test had been absurdly simple, so much so I began to wonder what he had in mind for me; because I had expected at least a moderately difficult one.

However, when the hall had cleared he called me in, and he didn't waste any time. 'Come with me,' he said. I followed him to a classroom at the end of the corridor. 'Go in there and report to Mr Cook.' I wasn't aware of it then, but from that moment my happy schooldays ceased to exist.

I entered, closed the door and approached the teacher, who was calling the roll. The silence in that room was such that one could have heard the proverbial pin drop.

Glancing idly at the class, I was astonished to see that every pupil was sitting bolt upright with arms folded and gazing fixedly to the front.

The teacher glanced at me, then he snarled, 'Go back to the door and wait until I call you.' I did so – and waited.

He finished the register then turned to me. 'Come here,' he barked. When I stood in front of him he said,

'Pupils do not enter my classroom without permission, do you understand?'

'Yes, Sir.'

'Right, what's your name?'

'Herbert, Sir.'

'Herbert what?'

'Samuel Herbert, Sir.'

There followed a short pause.

'Where have you come from?'

'The hall, Sir.'

'I know that, you fool, what school were you attending?'

'St Nicholas', Sir.'

He finished writing. 'Sit there,' he snapped, pointing to a desk at the front of the class, and immediately under his podium.

I sat down, folded my arms and assumed the expression of a sphinx. That was the first of many encounters I was to have with Mr Cook.

Dad only laughed when I poured out my tale of woe. 'It won't do you any harm,' were his words of comfort.

Chapter Twenty-Five

Situated in Marlborough Crescent was a cinema – the Palace Theatre. For a penny you could proceed upstairs to the gallery, where you either stood or sat on the floor and watched such beauties as Pearl White.

Two pence was charged for admittance to the aptly named pit, where you were given the doubtful luxury of a wooden form to sit on; added to which was the pleasure of being on the receiving end of a constant hail of orange peel, apple gowks and such like.

It was also advisable for those pit punters to carry umbrellas, because, due to the lack of toilets, the dirty sods in the gallery simply leaned over the balcony and drenched those below with a torrent of urine!

It really was a palace of variety, and many a young maiden was ruthlessly deflowered in its murky confines.

The owner of that palace – a man by the name of James Lowe – was an optimist; he had hoped to make his fortune. Realisation that his optimism was simply wishful thinking dawned on him one Saturday evening.

He had gone to great expense to acquire a Charlie Chaplin film (one of the first two-part efforts) and he was rubbing his hands with delight at the spectacle of a packed auditorium.

Just before the picture was about to start, he was heard yelling near the main door. He then made his way upstairs and in an anguished voice addressed the now packed audience; 'Ladies and gentlemen, the gallery is full, the pit is likewise, but there is fuck-all in the pay-box!'

With that, he turned, tripped and fell headlong down the stairs! Poor James, all the way to the Infirmary he babbled, 'Nowt in the pay-box, nowt in the pay-box!'

However, apart from a broken arm he was unhurt, but he closed the theatre for a month.

The reason for the shortage in takings was obvious. About an hour before the show started, some very dishonest lads had forced an upstairs window, and, because of the poor lighting, scores of villains were not spotted as they lay silent under the forms and clinging to the rafters.

As I said, James Lowe was an optimist and when he had recovered from his fall he installed better lighting before he re-opened the cinema.

Attendances though were not too good, but James had a brainwave.

To the surprise of the audience, there was flashed on the tatty old screen one Saturday evening the following notice:

> Ladies and Gentlemen, as from Monday,
> the price of admission will be:-
> Upstairs – one jam jar
> Downstairs – two jam jars

Don't laugh, dear reader, because jars were really accepted as entrance money. There was of course an acute shortage of those commodities immediately following the war.

Once again James rubbed his hands gleefully; the hall was packed every night and very soon there was a mountain of jars locked away in a big shed at the rear of the cinema.

Optimist he may have been, but by heaven he was thick! He didn't stop to wonder why there was a sudden increase in the audience figures after a few weeks. Nor did it occur to him that jars were plentiful – even though there was a shortage.

Yes, you have guessed it! Some hooligan had procured a key to the shed and as fast as the bottles were wheeled in at one end, they were promptly abstracted at the other. They were then flogged by the purloiners to prospective customers.

In effect, those bottles were going round and round in never decreasing circles!

But James was a glutton for punishment, as was proved by another announcement on the screen:

> Ladies and Gentlemen, as from Monday
> the price of admission will be:-
> Upstairs – one penny
> Downstairs – two pence
> And which thieving bugger pinched my jars?

He also had a sense of humour.

I was very glad though that the vicar never learned of the part I played in the matter of the missing bottles.

I include this story to emphasise a particular point, which is: without the stern, restraining hand of my father, I would have indulged in many similar escapades – even dishonest ones.

I didn't always escape scot-free though; I well remember an escapade for which I was to pay dearly.

About four weeks after my entry to Cambridge Street, I noticed four lads sharing out what appeared to be a cap full of money. I was acquainted with one of them and in answer to my nosy question he replied succinctly, 'Bull-walloping.'

I looked at him. 'Bull-walloping?'

'Aye – you know, driving the cattle from the sidings to the market.'

Then the penny dropped.

In those days there was a cattle market on Scotswood Road, a sheep market on what is now the Marlborough bus station and a pig market, which was opposite. Cattle were brought in railway trucks to sidings, which were located in Railway Street and Forth Banks.

There the beasts were collected by drovers and hustled to their respective market. 'So,' said that lad, 'We go to the sidings every Monday dinner time, which is the busiest, and ask the drovers if they need any help.'

'What happens then?' I asked.

'It's easy – all you do is walk behind the cattle and give them a whack now and again with a stick, and when they reach the market we get a tanner, or sometimes a bob!'

Well, it didn't sound too easy to me so I promptly forgot about it.

Then came the following Monday – a day that was to etched in my memory for all time.

'Want to come, kidder?'

'Come where?'

'You know – the sidings – bull-walloping.'

'No thanks,' I replied.

'Come on, it's only for an hour and you could make a few bob.'

I hesitated. The thought of earning a 'few bob' began to appeal to me. 'Right, I'll have a go,' I said. (Foolish boy.)

And so it was that at twelve noon I galloped down Rye Hill along with the other three boys en-route to Railway Street.

I hadn't even occurred to me that Mother would wonder where I had got to – oh no, my uppermost thought was a few bob!

What met my eyes at the sidings was a scene of absolute chaos. As the trucks were shunted in, the ramps were lowered and with many pokes with their sticks the drovers persuaded the reluctant beasts to leave their mobile pens. Then with much arm waving, screaming of oaths and prolific use of sticks, the drovers urged the beasts towards the exit. I suppose there would be about three dozen animals in each batch.

For quite some time I stood watching the antics of men and beasts, and the exciting prospect of earning a few bob was replaced by a feeling of apprehension.

I noticed that two of my companions had been 'engaged' by a drover and were busy urging a small herd towards the exit, but by that time I definitely was having second thoughts.

I was about to leave when I heard the remaining boy shouting and waving to me, so, somewhat reluctantly, I walked towards him. 'We've got a job,' he said. 'You stand there and stop them (the bulls) from going past you.'

I took up my position a few yards from the rear of the truck and gazed with no little trepidation at the snorting, snuffling beasts gazing out through the openings of the trucks.

Then the ramps were lowered and I watched as the first of the hairy brutes – which was adorned with a wicked looking pair of horns – made its way out.

It looked at me with a bloodshot, baleful eye. 'Shoo,' I squeaked. The bovine monstrosity showed its complete contempt for me – it turned its arse in my direction and deposited at my feet a pancake of brown stew.

Somewhat disconcerted, I again squeaked 'Shoo, shoo.' But I had to utter many more ineffectual squeaks before that future bottle of Bovril walked disdainfully in the desired direction.

Eventually, the required number of bulls having been disgorged, the driver prepared to move off. 'You two bring up the rear, I will lead them.' He then made his way up to the front, but after a few minutes and some more frantic arm waving, it became obvious that the cattle had no intention of leaving the sidings.

Anxiously, I saw that they were turning in my direction, and then with a gasp I watched as they broke into a gallop – straight for me! I had no wish to be trampled underfoot by those hairy horrors, so I bolted.

But almost too late I realised there was no place to run to. The entrance to the sidings from the other end was almost half a mile away and the whole area was bounded by a ten foot wall.

Terrified out of my wits, I jumped in between two of the rail trucks and watched as those bullocks thundered past.

Badly shaken, I hurried out of the sidings, and then I received another shock. I glanced at the cattle market clock, which, to my dismay, showed the time to be almost one-thirty – and I was due back at school at one forty-five.

There was little else I could do but gallop up Rye Hill and nip into the school cloakroom for a quick wash before afternoon assembly began. I just made it.

Whilst I was somewhat concerned as to Ma's reaction if she should find out where I had been, my immediate reaction was one of relief to have made the roll-call. But trouble was soon forthcoming.

It happened midway through a written essay, when Mr Cook, who was walking about keeping an eye on us, stopped suddenly beside me. Glancing up at him I saw his nose twitching – then he began to sniff audibly.

He then looked under my seat – and so did I. I groaned inwardly when I realised why he was sniffing – my boots were plastered with cow shit and because the room was so warm, it had began to ferment. The result? An abominable pong was permeating the whole class-room. I awaited the worst.

'You disgusting creature,' he snarled as he grabbed me by the scruff and literally lifted me to the front of the class.

Sick at heart, I looked at an outraged Mr Cook, who, strangely enough, was finding it difficult to speak.

I also became aware of some half-stifled laughter from the class.

Then, after a few seconds spluttering, Cook seized me by the lug-hole, rushed me out of the room and into the hall, where I received the punishment I had simply asked for. Further to that he ordered me home, and as I walked sorrowfully down the stairs I reached behind to massage my stinging rear end – it was then that I realised why the class had tittered – there was a six inch hole in my trousers, which meant that they had been given a birds-eye view of my lily-white bum!

I had time to dwell on the disastrous outcome of my intended 'bull-walloping' as I made my way home, and I still had my Mother to face!

Forgive me if I draw a veil over what happened later.

Chapter Twenty-Six

It is true to say that the closing months of 1921 were to see the end of my silly and often dangerous escapades.

I think the reason was due not so much to the thrashing Mother gave me (it may have helped) after the bull-walloping incident, but rather more to the fact that all my friends' parents had now clamped down on their activities. But there were other factors; for instance, Terry, who had settled down in his first job, had forgone all the mischievous pranks in which he used to participate. In fact, for almost two years our active friendship ceased.

Billy was also on the point of taking up employment, whilst George, Bobby and Peter, like myself, had had their wings clipped.

There was little if any change in our home conditions, but because Dad was still in regular employment and Fred was enthusiastically plugging away as a riveter's apprentice, we were, financially, a great deal better off.

But oh, that damned house! It was a permanent battle against damp and vermin, and I have to say a losing one.

Dad, who now drank very little, was trying like hell to get enough money saved up to enable him to apply for one of the houses that were now available – but for which at least three months' rent in advance was demanded.

To return to Fred for a moment. He was continuing to sleep with his friend in the home of that good lady caretaker of the boys' school.

I wasn't too sure that he was absolutely dedicated to his job in the shipyard, but I was perfectly sure of his determination to get out of that damned Avenue. But, most surprisingly, he often spoke about joining the army. 'There,' he would say, 'I will get fresh air, plenty of food and a bed with no cockroaches in it.'

Sadly, as he knew only too well, his suspect chest would prove to be an effective barrier against attaining that particular ambition.

As for myself, well, the first four months at Cambridge Street had been almost unbearable, due in the main to Mr Cook's attitude towards me. There was no doubt that I was his main target, because, obviously, he had not forgotten the bull-walloping incident. There were times when I only had to blink to receive a couple of the best. In fact, so obvious was his dislike of me and so numerous were the beltings I received, that many of my classmates begged me to tell my parents what was going on – but I wouldn't do so.

I couldn't understand why he should treat me so, because I was working hard and getting first-class marks.

But the turning point was to come in an unexpected manner – albeit a painful one.

I have not, as yet, mentioned the school choir, so perhaps now is the time to do so. It was formed after I had begun schooling at Cambridge Street and, discovering that I had a good voice, the music master, Mr Pratt, persuaded me to join. (I would have joined anything that got me away from Mr Cook!) We practised in the Assembly Hall every Tuesday and Friday, usually during the last hour of school time.

This incident I am going to relate took place on a Friday afternoon, shortly before my thirteenth birthday.

We had returned to the classroom after the afternoon break and, as I normally did, I asked Mr Cook's permission to leave the room and join the choir. I got the usual curt nod in response – so off I went. I was about to enter the hall when I suddenly remembered I had left my book of music in my desk.

'Hurry up then,' said Mr Pratt in answer to my request to return for it. I ran back to my classroom, opened the door and hurriedly entered. Then I stopped in my tracks, because I realised I had made a cardinal error – I hadn't knocked.

I looked at Mr Cook, who was glaring at me with his now familiar sour look.

'Why didn't you knock?'

'Sorry, Sir, I forgot through being in a hurry.'

'Then this will teach you to remember—'

Do you know that swine gave me four whacking strokes with a cane, two on each hand.

'Now return to the choir,' he snarled.

Had I been a bigger and stronger lad I would have committed the most serious of crimes, I would have clouted him. Certainly I was in no mood now for singing – I was having a hell of a job keeping the tears back.

Acting purely on impulse I walked to my desk, sat down and placed my stinging hands in my armpits.

'I said join the choir!'

I looked at him and shook my head.

'Do you hear me boy?'

I ignored him.

That was the beginning of the most frightening experience of my young life. He grabbed me by the collar and dragged me to the front of the class, where he attempted to lay me across a seat. I resisted him, which enraged him even more. He began laying about my shoulders with that bloody cane and heaven only knows what would have happened if Mr Pratt had not entered – he was looking for me. I heard him say something like 'Good God', but I was now past caring. To have to suffer such pain and humiliation for a trivial offence proved too much and the tears began to run down my face. I galloped down the stairs, left the school and made my way home – to discover Dad there. (He'd had to come home because of heavy rain.)

'What's wrong with you?' he quietly asked.

I couldn't answer – but held my hands out. He looked with anger at my now swollen fingers then rose from his chair, donned his jacket and said, 'Come on!' He almost ran to the school, and when I guided him to the Head's study he knocked quite forcibly on the door.

Now, the most remarkable feature of this story is the astonishingly abrupt manner in which it was concluded.

The door was opened by the Head, who showed no surprise when Dad introduced himself. 'Yes, please come in.' He then looked at me. 'You remain there for a while.' But before the door was closed I caught sight of Mr Pratt and Mr Cook seated in the study.

Some twenty minutes later, Dad emerged followed by the Head, whose name incidentally was Mr Bastin, and it was he who spoke. 'Report to me tomorrow before the morning assembly.' And with that Dad marched off.

I was never to learn what transpired in the Head's study; Dad's only comment was, 'You shouldn't have any more trouble.'

I stood in the Head's study the following morning wondering what was going to happen, but he simply said, 'I am placing you in 7X.' This was a special class consisting of no more than a dozen boys who were considered to be brainy and had a year or less to do before leaving. It was a privileged class and the subjects taught (by the Head) were mostly slightly advanced Maths and English.

Some three months later Mr Bastin collapsed and died from a heart attack. His successor? Mr Cook, of course.

Chapter Twenty-Seven

Mr Pratt, our music teacher, was quite a character: he was a tubby little man with a great sense of humour, who derived as much enjoyment from conducting the choir as the choir enjoyed singing. He was the cheese to Mr Cook's chalk.

Apart from his uncanny skill at making singers out of 'bullfrogs' (his pet name for those budding singers who tended to croak), he was an accomplished pianist.

His repertoire was amazingly versatile: he could render a nocturne by Chopin with the same ease as a popular tune. It wasn't unusual for him – after giving the choir a gruelling half hour – to sit at the piano and enthral us with a display of his prowess.

It was because of him that I developed a passion for 'good music', and during the summer months I would invariably make my way to Elswick Park on Sunday afternoons just to sit and absorb the music of various brass bands. And that brings to mind a delightful little story.

I was returning home after listening to one of those musical treats, and running through my head was a particularly catchy tune that had been played and when I entered the kitchen I was quite unconsciously humming it aloud.

'What is that you are singing?' asked Dad.

'Oh, something the band played this afternoon,' I replied casually.

'Do you know what it is called?'

'No.'

He looked at me thoughtfully, then went to a drawer that contained his personal property, unlocked it and brought out an album, one of three he possessed, but the only one he had never opened to us. He opened it, and to my amazement I saw that instead of a display of photographs, there was a musical box, a kind of miniature barrel organ.

'I don't know whether it will play or not,' he mused, as he groped around for the key. He found the key and very carefully wound it up and closed the lid. Then to my delight it began playing the same piece of music I had listened to that afternoon, and which had haunted me since.

I was absolutely fascinated by the tinkling tones of that exquisite piece of workmanship, and I watched regretfully when he re-locked the box and replaced it in the drawer.

Then with a smile he said, 'That musical box was made in Italy more than a hundred years ago, and it was presented to my grandfather when he retired. The music it plays are excerpts from *The Gondoliers*, a Gilbert and Sullivan opera.' (Sadly, as I wrote earlier, that particular album disappeared along with the other two.)

However, to continue my story concerning Mr Pratt.

Besides being a master on the piano, he had one very favourite hobby, and that was drama. He had a permanent group of about twelve players – who were usually final year pupils – and with unfailing regularity he would write a play, produce it and then present it to an audience consisting mainly of pupils' parents. It cannot be denied that the plays were always well received – due mostly to his own infectious enthusiasm.

I may have had a good voice – and I knew I was quite intelligent – but I was not endowed with the ability necessary to be an actor, and it took a rib-tickling episode to convince Mr Pratt that I was a better singer than actor.

Do any of you remember Empire Day? No matter.
In those days this little island of ours was a great power.
We not only ruled the waves but also three parts of the
world's land, and on one particular day of every year –
Empire Day – the country would celebrate it's power by
flag-waving, speeches, and never-ending martial music,
and added to that innumerable plays would be performed
throughout the country extolling England's might.

And so it was in 1921 that our Mr Pratt decided to try
and surpass everything he had ever achieved by writing a
play about Empire Day.

It was quite a simple play really – about a young cynic
who, after viewing the bunting with a jaundiced eye,
would thereupon sneer and make derogatory comments.
He in turn would suffer wrathful verbal attacks from a
player representing Britannia and from others representing the armed forces.

It was to be a gala afternoon: the play would be preceded by choir-singing – with some solo efforts from
your humble and a girl singer.

All went smoothly during rehearsals and Mr Pratt was
waxing eloquently, but then his luck ran out when, on
the morning of the great day, he received a note from the
boy who was to act the cynic – he was ill!

Poor Mr Pratt, after many abortive attempts to obtain
a volunteer replacement he finally came to see me. 'You
are my last hope,' he wailed.

Well, like I said, I was no actor, but the anguished look
on his face overcame my commonsense – I agreed to
take over the part. Having watched the rehearsals many
times, I was sure I could manage to spout the necessary
lines without much difficulty.

The whole cast had a hurried final rehearsal with each
of them dressed in their outfits. Mr Pratt had decided
that the cynic should be garbed in colonial dress, and
his idea of that was a drill shirt, short trousers and, of all
things, puttees!

Mother surprised me when she declared her intention to come and 'watch the fun!' (She must have been psychic.)

The curtain rose to an absolutely packed hall: there were mothers and fathers, a load of sceptical pupils and some rather pompous looking officials.

There was tremendous applause when the choir – and yours truly – had concluded the choral lines and there was a short interval before the play began.

With his usual ingenuity, Mr Pratt had erected a stage – complete with wings – and my position during the opening was behind one of them.

I well remember the first words I had to utter; 'Plays, songs and speeches, what's its all about?'

And so the curtain rose, to reveal the actors standing in a line with Britannia in the centre, and I was in my allotted spot in the wings.

It was really great! Britannia made a patriotic speech (applause), then the soldier, the airman and finally the sailor made similar speeches and each received generous applause. My cue had arrived.

I took a deep breath, stepped smartly forward and a split second later I flew through the air and landed on my belly at the feet of Britannia! I distinctly heard some titters from the audience, but when I looked up to Britannia and bawled, 'What's it all about, eh?' the hall erupted. I simply had to carry on, and the audience, realising perhaps my embarrassment, quietened down – then I finished my piece.

I felt sick, and I knew that my face resembled a beetroot. Nevertheless, the audience very generously applauded my effort and I then turned smartly and began to walk off the stage. I had only taken one step and then, horror of horrors, I stumbled again and did another belly-flapper! That was too much for the audience, who began to roll about laughing. Mr Pratt can't have been too happy but he picked me up, patted me on the back and said simply, 'Well done.'

Suddenly he pursed his lips and said, 'Look at that!' He pointed to my feet. I looked, and to my chagrin I saw that one of the puttees resembled an unwound roll of toilet paper. Of course I didn't realise that I had one foot on the end of it when I made my ridiculous flying entrance.

It took a long time before I was allowed to forget that experience, but, funnily enough, it had served one useful purpose. You see, and I freely admit this – I was developing a swollen head. Because I was a good singer, brainy and a member of the elite class, I thought at times that I was the bee's knees. Well that incident literally brought me down to earth with a bump.

The moral of this story is – should one ever develop into a pompous ass, then one should ensure that one's laces are fastened.

Chapter Twenty-Eight

I stood, looking at my enemy – Mr Cook. Without any preamble he said, 'I have had a visit from your mother.'

Well, did I look astonished!

'My mother?'

'Yes,' curtly as was his wont!

I waited, very, very puzzled.

Then he continued, 'You are having difficulty with your homework.'

I then realised he was making a statement and not asking a question.

'A little, Sir.'

He looked at me for the first time since I entered his study, 'Your parents are asking for advice.'

I didn't answer.

After an awkward pause he went on. 'There is little I can do, but in view of your being nominated for a scholarship later this year, I can arrange for you to attend evening classes twice a week, thus cutting out the home-work.'

Well, one must give the very Devil his due if he deserves or merits it, and I had to appreciate Cook's thoughtfulness on this occasion. (And the nomination for a scholarship came as a complete surprise!)

So what could I say?

'Thank you, Sir.'

I began my evening classes the following week at Cruddas Park School, and thereby hangs another story – one that could have resulted in tragedy but actually finished on a hilarious note.

I was making my way home one evening from the school, and, as I walked up Rye Hill, I saw Terry speaking to a girl we both knew. Naturally, I stood and chatted for a while to both of them. It was early February and it was quite a gloomy night.

Now, I was standing on the pavement with my back to The Avenue when, suddenly, we heard voices yelling and screaming, but there was nothing unusual in that so we just ignored it.

But the yells were coming nearer and I was about to comment on it when I became aware of strange drumming sound, and as I started to turn out of curiosity I received a blow like a ram-rod on my backside. Then I was lifted into the air and deposited some yards away.

Shocked, I vaguely heard Terry and the girl shouting and, looking around, I saw the reason. Standing a few yards away from me was a massive bull! It was snorting and pawing the ground as only bulls can when angry.

With a yell of terror I scrambled to safety inside some garden railings, then the bull made off.

A few minutes later three or four men, obviously drovers, came running towards us.

'Anybody seen a bull?' shouted one of them.

'Aye,' said Terry, who was laughing uproariously. 'It's just been here and shoved its fuckin' horn up Sammy's arse!'

Reproachfully I looked at him and then he said, 'Have you seen your trousers?'

I looked, and to my amazement I saw they were ripped open right across my backside.

Dolefully I made my way home, and who could blame my parents for their sceptic reaction when I informed them I had been gored by a bull!

But the ugly bruise on my back confirmed my story and also emphasised how narrow a squeak I'd had from serious injury.

'Why,' said Dad later, 'didn't the bull stick its horn in your grinning pal's backside?' (He meant Terry.)

So, for the second time in my life I suffered from the unwanted attentions of cattle, and I almost became a vegetarian.

Chapter Twenty-Nine

One memorable event of early 1922 was that my voice broke, and, as a result, my choir-singing career came to a halt.

That, however, did not prevent me from attending church and I took advantage of my non-singing by assisting the organist. Incidentally, the organ was old and in a rather dilapidated condition, and had the unhappy knack of developing tantrums at the most awkward and unexpected times.

The wind was generated by hand-operated bellows, and it was necessary to begin pumping some two or three minutes before the organist began to play. (And I can assure you that whoever had the tedious job of working the pump handle up and down would have aching arms when he finished.)

I began to take a great interest in the playing of it, and, providing I could procure someone to pump, I began teaching myself to play simple hymn tunes. They were most enjoyable interludes and very gratifying when I became proficient enough to play with both hands.

But I never really harboured any great desire to take up organ playing seriously – as was suggested by the organist. Besides, I was already doing as much studying as I could take.

I think that my enthusiasm for organ playing began to wane somewhat following an embarrassing episode. It happened at a wedding, when the daughter of one of our sidesmen was to be married. She was a regular worshipper at our church and I knew her very well.

Despite having planned a quiet wedding, she had decided to have our organist play the Wedding March for her. At his request, I readily agreed to pump the bellows for him, so I turned up about an hour before the ceremony just to grease the vital parts and ensure everything was in working order. Then – calamity!

About thirty minutes before the ceremony was due to begin, the vicar arrived with the news that the organist was ill. 'Then she will have to do without,' I said to him.

He added, 'Yes, I am afraid so, but it's a pity and she will be so disappointed.'

He was really upset as I watched him descend the stairs to the vestry. I closed the lids on the keyboards and then made my way down –he was waiting for me at the bottom. He looked at me as though searching for some inspiration and then he pointed his finger at me, 'You can do it.'

'Do what?' I asked.

'Play the organ laddie – play the organ.'

'Did you say play the organ?'

'Yes, laddie, yes.'

I gave a hearty guffaw but something in his face stopped me, and when I looked at him carefully my body developed a goose-pimple rash because I realised the fool was serious. I gasped, then sputtered, 'You don't mean —'

'Oh yes, I do, I have heard you play hymns and the Wedding March is similar.'

This was ridiculous.

'No,' I said, 'I can't do it.'

'Of course you can, there's nothing to it.'

'Then you play it!'

'I can't play a note.'

'I'm sorry Vicar; I shall make a fool of myself.'

I was determined not to play that damned organ, but I didn't reckon on having to cope with the old buffer's cajolery, because, believe me, when he cajoled he could relieve a monkey of his nuts!

'Anyway, I don't feel too well,' I moaned.

'Oh rubbish, it is just an attack of nerves,' he said soothingly.

'And there is no one here to pump the thing,' I said triumphantly.

'Oh yes there is, Mr Jackson (the curate) will do that for you.'

Not only was I beaten and in the depths of despair, but I was also having trouble with my bladder when, unresistingly, I let him turn me around and push me gently but firmly back up the stairs – there were only a few minutes to go. I turned my head skywards. 'For heaven's sake, help me,' I whispered.

With sweat running down my face I sat at the organ, awaiting the arrival of the bride. I glanced at the curate, who gave me an encouraging nod, and at that moment the bride entered the church.

With a feeling of dismay I realised that Mr Jackson should have been pumping like merry hell, and even though I hissed 'Pump!' I knew that a catastrophe was about to occur.

Yes I know, I should never have allowed myself to be cajoled into such a ridiculous situation, because, comparatively speaking, I knew damn all about organ music.

Admittedly, the Wedding March can be played in a simple manner, even by a novice, but not on a stuttering, unreliable relic of an organ such as that one.

The bride has just reached the aisle when the slumbering beast, whose keys I was frantically pressing, suddenly came to life, and dear God it was simply awful.

Like an overfed grampus, it emitted an enormous belch, which was followed by a gurgling that gave the impression it was being strangled. But the red-faced curate, who was now pumping furiously, must have seen the funny side – he was laughing his damn head off!

Then, at last, bloated with enough wind to float an airship, the brute relented and blew out my interpretation of the March.

I began to feel a little more relaxed, and with the knowledge that my ordeal would soon be over, I began depressing the keys with great gusto.

Out of the corner of my eye I could see the curate pumping away merrily, and, quite unconsciously, I began to keep time with the up and down movement of his arm, with the result, of course, that the music was at least three times quicker than it should have been.

Having to concentrate on the keyboard, I hadn't a clue as to what had happened, but when I peeped over the balcony I saw that the few guests who were there had their hands over their mouths, and I also noticed that the father of the bride was glaring at me with undisguised hostility. I got the feeling that all was not well down below, and when the curate, in between bouts of laughter, said, 'I don't think that went too well,' I decided to beat it, smartish!

I didn't return to church until weeks later, hoping that the unhappy episode had been forgotten. Well, it hadn't been, but, to my surprise and relief, I learned that it was being remembered as a most humorous interlude.

Even the father of the bride had seen the funny side after all, because he later said to me, 'You were playing at such speed my daughter had to do the quick march and I had to trot almost to keep up with her!'

I gave a wide berth to that brute of an organ after that.

Chapter Thirty

There are none so blind as those who cannot see exactly what is going on around them – even with perfect sight. I have used that abstract statement to illustrate how blind I was during the early part of 1922.

I suppose I could be forgiven, because, during that period, I was on cloud nine, and the reasons for my starry-eyed state were, firstly, the anticipation of a trip to Paris with the Scouts, for which I was hoarding every penny I could scrounge, secondly, I was doing exceedingly well at school, which was then much more pleasurable because of Mr Cook's slightly more tolerant attitude towards me and, thirdly, I had recommenced my friendship with Irene, my schoolgirl friend.

Apart from an occasional brief meeting on a Sunday, I had seen little of her since she moved to a different school; and I have to admit that I began to develop thoughts concerning her that made me feel ashamed.

Well, I was a strong, sturdy lad, and, like most youths who dwelt in The Avenue, I had assimilated, almost at first-hand, all the knowledge needed to understand the facts of life.

Added to that was the realisation I had reached puberty, and as Irene was growing into a lovely girl, it was inevitable that my thoughts would deviate from the scrupulously moral.

(And she liked me too!)

I suppose my feelings for her could be deemed as calf-love, but I also had a tremendous amount of respect for her, and I always looked forward with a great deal of pleasure to those long walks we took together.

Oddly enough, it was that same friendship which was to herald the first of many black clouds that would plunge me into the depths of depression during the months that lay ahead.

Irene imparted the news one Sunday evening when I met her after church. I couldn't help but notice that she was not as cheerful as usual, and she told me the reason immediately. I blinked a little when she said, 'I won't be seeing you again after tonight.'

'What's wrong?' I asked, mystified.

'We are moving to Whitley Bay next week,' she replied.

'Oh,' I said.

There was really nothing more to be said so I walked her home, said a simple 'Goodbye' and that was it.

But dammit, calf-love or no, some little time was to elapse before the memory of her began to fade.

It began to dawn on me during the middle of that year that my father was staying away from work rather a lot, and when I asked him why, he answered, 'Oh, I just have an infection of the throat that's proving difficult to get rid of.'

I thought no more of it; after all, lots of people get sore throats.

In the meantime, I had been having further brushes with the detestable Thug.

I had steadfastly continued to ignore him and his taunts, which had become more frequent. He had in fact made it known to all and sundry that he was going to get 'that toffee-nosed twat' (me) before he was much older.

And it also meant that sooner or later I would have to go against my father's wishes and do battle in the streets.

It was my good friends Terry and Billy who really started the countdown to what was to prove a bloody battle.

To my surprise, Billy told me he was building a small boxing ring in a back room of his uncle's house, which was on Cambridge Street, and why didn't I go along and take boxing lessons from his uncle, who had been an accomplished amateur boxer in his day. Well, up to then, my dealings with the noble art of self-defence had been through the medium of characters in *Comic Cuts*. Besides, I was almost certain Dad would not approve, but I promised to consider it.

Two nights later, I turned up for my first lesson. Why? I had just learned that Fred had been the victim of a brutal attack by Thug's brother – an eighteen year old with the same evil characteristics as his younger brother.

I was particularly upset when I was informed by witnesses that Fred had been attacked because he'd had the temerity to defend me against the verbal abuse being indulged in by the two brothers, and in doing so my quiet, inoffensive brother paid the penalty.

Even though a shocked doctor had described Fred's injuries as appalling, and had recommended police action, Dad wouldn't hear of it, and that, I thought, was wrong, because it meant that Thug and his family – apart from their sneering contempt for us – wouldn't hesitate to have a go at us whenever they felt like it.

And Mother didn't mince her words; 'What are you trying to do with our lads – turn them into punch bags?'

But Dad remained unmoved; in fact, with great emphasis, he repeated what he had said a year previously: 'I will not tolerate street fighting. It doesn't follow that because we are forced to live in this area we have to act like those thugs. And that is my last word.'

'Dad?' I said.

'Yes.'

I gulped a couple of times. 'May I take up boxing?'

'What?'

I repeated my request – with another couple of gulps. To my astonishment he turned and said, 'Now that's more like it – boxing is a hard but clean sport – yes, of course you can.'

He didn't ask particulars and I thought it best not to enlighten him. That's how I became the third member of Billy's club (there were never any more).

And so, what little time I had to spare was spent in that little boxing ring, and for weeks I had the bloody daylights knocked out of me; but I learned to fight, and the time would come when I was to feel eternally grateful to Billy and his uncle.

Chapter Thirty-One

I was next. The boys had preceded me into Mr Cook's study and by the expressions on their faces when they left, the proceedings had been anything but pleasant.

And so I stood facing the scowling man, wondering what was in store for me.

You see, two weeks earlier, we, the elite class, had sat a test paper, a sort of preliminary for the scholarship test, and we were now being given the results.

I waited patiently and then he spoke. 'Did you find this test difficult?'

'Yes, Sir.'

'You did quite well —'

I didn't answer.

Perhaps my apparent indifference got under his skin a little because he barked, 'Well, do you wish to go to a grammar school or not?'

That, of course, was Dad's most earnest hope and I answered truthfully, 'Why, yes, Sir.'

He ended the interview with some instructions and a warning not to let up.

The day following the interview was the beginning of the summer holidays and I was to attend Bath Lane School on the first Monday after they ended – along with only four other boys from my class.

As was to be expected, my parents – especially Dad

– were absolutely delighted at my selection, and Fred, rather gruffly, said, 'Good for you young'un, keep at it.'

I was determined not to disappoint them. But my own happiness at that time was tempered by an awareness of some little deterioration in home life. This was mainly due to Dad's enforced absence from work because of his troublesome throat infection, and whatever sick benefit he received was a mere trifle.

I also knew full well how saddened he was at having to use the money he had been saving in order to make ends meet. But he was constantly cheerful, even though I heard him say to Mother, 'It's going to be damned hard if I don't get back to work soon.'

One other aspect of my life was proceeding on its merry, if painful, way. I had begun to learn that boxing was not for the faint-hearted.

My first few weeks at Billy's 'gymnasium' were spent mostly sitting on my arse – having been knocked there by my grinning pals.

But I learned quickly, and very soon I could dish it out equally well. But, no matter how hard we punched each other (and those two sods could really punch), the evening activities always ended with laughter all round.

Both Terry and Billy were now working for their living, and as a consequence I saw little of them, but that had not diminished our friendship in any way.

There comes to mind an incident in which they were both involved – one that took place as we were making our way home after a session in the ring. Although it didn't concern me and has no real bearing on my story, I am relating it simply to illustrate just how much *hidden* brutality prevailed in The Avenue.

The story concerns two boys – twins aged sixteen – and their sisters aged fifteen and seventeen. Along with their mother, they lived in a two-bedroom tenement on the lower part of The Avenue. They were nicely dressed girls, quite attractive too, but oh so reserved.

Like all other girls of their age, they had to run the gauntlet of wolf whistles and even displays of obscene gestures. But they seldom, if ever, showed any reaction, except for one lad who never failed to raise a smile on their faces – particularly the older girl. (You have guessed who of course – Terry.)

Their twin brothers were both unpleasant young brutes, in fact they had done periods of corrective training for assaulting their mother.

As we made our way along Cambridge Street, Terry spotted the two girls coming towards us, and as they were about to pass us we noticed that the older girl's face was quite badly bruised. Terry was shocked by her appearance, and I think it was the genuine concern in his voice when he asked what had happened that prompted her to stop and answer him. 'Just a slight accident,' she replied.

Before he could make any further comment there began an incident, one which was to have consequences so far reaching as to be almost unbelievable.

Glancing idly around, I suddenly spotted the girl's twin brothers walking quickly towards us. Both Terry and Billy had their backs turned and were unaware of the twins' approach.

I had an uneasy feeling that something unpleasant was about to happen – and it did – with incredible swiftness. The twins elbowed my friends aside and one of them delivered a terrific punch to the older girl's face. She screamed then fell to the ground – her brother followed her – having been put there by Billy and Terry!

And it was whilst they were methodically beating the twins almost to death that further trouble arrived, in the shape of two massive policemen. In normal circumstances the police would simply administer their own brand of punishment to street fighters and that would either be a good kick up the arse or a belt across the lughole. But the condition of the girl – who was still on the ground – called for more serious action. And so it was that Terry, Billy and the twins were whipped away to the local 'nick' while the older girl was taken to the hospital.

Had that been the end of the story I would not have written it.

You see, whilst receiving treatment, the older girl unburdened herself to the doctors, who then discovered she was three months pregnant. And the father? One of the twins!

The poor girl had been raped repeatedly by those animals, and had also been brutally battered in the process.

And the outcome? Twelve years each in prison for the twins and a ticking off for Billy and Terry.

In such crowded conditions, where it is almost impossible to segregate the sexes, the baser instincts of many men, aye, and women, can prove strong enough to overcome decency and that's what I meant by hidden brutality.

Chapter Thirty-Two

As the months passed, it became increasingly obvious that our living standards were reaching a low level.

There had been little or no improvement in Dad's throat condition, and it was a bitter blow to him when he was informed that specialist advice and treatment were necessary. But he was as much distressed by having, once again, to apply for Parish Relief – no doubt remembering the previous humiliating experiences.

But despite all that, the seriousness of the situation did not register with me, because I was deeply engrossed in rag collecting – the much-looked-forward-to trip to Paris with the Scouts was only a mere two months away and I had managed to save only half of the money I needed.

However, with the coming of the summer holidays I had a great deal of time in which to indulge in cash-raising efforts, and they were many and varied.

At four-thirty every evening I would purchase two-dozen copies of the *Evening Chronicle* from the *Chronicle* offices, for two shillings and then proceed on a mad dash through the streets to try and sell them. If I succeeded (and sometimes I didn't) I would earn one shilling profit.

Early mornings and afternoons I could be found outside the Central Station, looking for passengers who were over-laden with luggage; of course I had to be rather servile, you know, touching the forelock and saying parrot-like, 'Carry your bag, Sir?' I seldom failed to get at least three or four jobs, such as the woman who gave me a bag that weighed a bloody ton, and I humped it right to the Haymarket. When we reached her hotel she dug into her bag and into my eager hand she placed a two-penny bar of chocolate!

Similarly there was a man who gave me his heavy golf bag to carry. It wasn't a long journey, just to Clayton Street. When we arrived at his hotel he reached inside his inside pocket and brought out a small case (I had visions of a note coming), he then withdrew from the case a cigar and handed it to me. 'Don't make yourself sick,' he said.

Then there were the grumpy travel-weary individuals whose response was usually 'piss off!' All in all though, if one was prepared to take the good with the bad, it was possible to earn at least ten shillings per day.

Not bad!

Being busy with all those activities meant that my church attendances were only of an occasional nature – much to the displeasure of the vicar. But, as I pointed out, my voice was still somewhat cracked, and I wasn't too keen on just 'making up the number'. Anyway, I was regularly attending the confirmation classes, and with that he had to be content.

★ ★ ★

It happened during the third week of my holidays – an incident that was to change the course of my whole life.

I shall never forget that particular Monday when I sat having my tea with the family.

It had suddenly occurred to Mother that Fred was a little late in getting home from work. 'Probably had to wait for a tram,' observed Dad. We finished tea, and, as Mother was clearing the table, there came a thunderous knocking at the door. I opened it and beheld a policeman.

'Your father in?' Hearing that Dad came to the door.
'Mr Herbert?'

'Yes.'

'I am sorry Mr Herbert but your son Fred has met with an accident; he's in the Royal Victoria Infirmary.

This was an absolute shocker! My parents hurriedly dressed and made off with all speed to the Infirmary, only to be told that Fred was sleeping following an operation on a broken leg. They were not allowed to see him, but having been assured there was nothing to worry about they returned home.

I know they spent a very anxious night, but they were at the Infirmary the following morning when they learned that Fred's leg was badly fractured and his arm and ribs had suffered some damage. And yet, even with those injuries, he was considered to be very lucky, because, after falling forty feet down a ship's hold, he landed on a man at the bottom.

Nevertheless, it was a cruel blow to Fred, more so considering his previous spell in hospital. In a lesser way it was a blow to Mother, who would be deprived of his very welcome weekly wage for many months ahead.

But I had an uneasy feeling that somehow I was to be personally affected by it all.

My fears were confirmed some days later, when, following an argument with Mother, I was left shattered and bitterly angry.

It amounted to the decision that I could not go to Paris.

I looked angrily at Mother. 'Why not?' I asked.

'How much money have you saved?'

'Ten pounds,' I replied.

'We cannot help you now.'

'You don't have to, I can raise the rest myself.'

'You realise that your father won't return to work for a long time?'

'Yes – but—'

'And that Fred will also be off work for months?'

'You mean you want my money?'

She looked at me and said, 'Yes, it will come in very useful.'

I felt as though I was choking; quite truthfully I had at that moment lost all respect for my parents. I had looked forward with great eagerness to the trip, and to achieve it I had ran myself almost ragged raising the money. Then, almost at the last moment, I had to suffer cruel disappointment. It was more than I could take.

I was unable to speak as I handed her the money and left the house.

I walked for hours, alone, round and round Elswick Park, dwelling bitterly on the events of that afternoon.

There was a further surprise in store for me when I arrived home shortly after tea – Fred had unexpectedly been sent home and he was lying on the settee looking pale and wan. But I was so fed up I gave him only a cursory glance.

I refused my tea and while I was washing myself, Mother asked where I was going. 'To the Scouts,' I answered, abruptly.

She continued talking to me but I was so full of resentment I barely heard a word she said.

'Aren't you going to put your uniform on?' she asked.

'No.'

'Why not?'

I looked at her, sadly almost with hatred, 'I am not going to wear it again,' I replied. And with that I left.

It wasn't easy telling the scoutmaster that I no longer wished to be considered for the trip, that I did not want to go and that my scouting days were over. And so they were, because I never returned.

Maybe some of you who read this will think that I acted in an over-emotional and spiteful manner, that I had not considered the straitened circumstances in which we were living, and that it would have been morally wrong to spend the money on a trip to Paris.

My answer to that would be this – I reacted in just the same way as any other fourteen year old who'd had a dream destroyed. Had I not been selected to go on the trip then I would not have saved any money. It would not have cost my parents one half-penny, therefore I could not have embarrassed them in any way. That was my reasoning at the time.

In retrospect my reasoning was right and justified, but only because I was completely unaware of the real seriousness that prevailed at the time – and shortage of money was only part of it.

Something else that surprised me was Dad's attitude. I was aware that he had been ordered not to use his voice under any circumstances for at least two months, but I was extremely upset by his (apparent) total indifference to the unhappy affair.

I was greatly appeased, however, when at last he mentioned it (or wrote it). I was having a last-minute swot for the scholarship exam – which was only two days hence – when he took my pencil and wrote on a piece of paper, 'Cheer up son, Paris will always be there!'
Well at least he understood how I felt.

But he was never to know that the agony of remorse would almost tear me apart when at last I learned the whole truth some little time later. It was a revelation that seared my very soul – and all the money in the world would not have comforted me.

Chapter Thirty-Three

Many changes had taken place in The Avenue by the time 1922 came to an end – in its population I mean. Most of the elderly people, who had somehow survived for so many years, had gone to a much more peaceful abode up above, but a new generation had been born – and sometimes reared – in that festering cesspool, before the authorities decided to take remedial action.

The conditions in my own home had worsened almost to crisis. As had happened during a previous difficult period, everything that was pawnable was now in 'Uncle's'.

Fred, who could do little but rest on the settee, was understandably irritable. His inability to do anything to help worried him tremendously. But his plight was eased by that good-natured lady in whose house he had been sleeping, because she insisted that he be taken there and remain until his leg healed.

We were now fully dependent on Parish Relief, meagre though it was, and no matter how hard Mother tried, she found it impossible to provide us with more than the bare necessities. Bread and margarine was once again the order of the day – dinners were a luxury.

You know, it was impossible not to feel sorry for her whilst she stood in the local Co-op ordering her few groceries, and in full view of other customers, self-consciously tendering a food voucher in payment.

I cannot but deny that during that period she had an almost unbearably heavy cross to bear, which she did with uncomplaining dignity.

One bright note during that depressing time was my success at the scholarship exam. I received the news from Mr Cook about a month later, and strangely for him, he condescended to offer me his congratulations.

Of course my parents were delighted, as were my friends, and some of the more decent neighbours even wished me well. It seemed that the passing of a scholarship by a boy from The Avenue had hitherto been unheard of.

But of all the good wishes I received, none pleased me more than those from a delighted Fred. And yet he made a rather odd comment, which was, 'Whatever happens, you must go to college.'

I pondered for a while, wondering exactly what he meant, then I forgot about it.

Exciting though the winning of the scholarship was, it also brought problems; there was the question of uniform and other necessities, which I well knew were beyond the reach of my parents.

However, after much deliberation, Mother decided to ask advice from Mr Cook, who, once again to my surprise, agreed to help by recommending me to the Education Committee as an exceptional case for assistance.

We were equally surprised when they agreed to assist in the purchase of whatever was needed. I had elected to attend Rutherford Grammar School, so I was all set.

And so it was that I stood facing Mr Cook for the last time on a grey December afternoon; his words to me were few, but I never forgot them. 'If you work hard, there is no reason why you should not do well in the field of literature.'

Thank you, Sir, and goodbye!

★ ★ ★

Christmas of 1922 was another of those hard-up, miserable affairs to which we had become accustomed, and one best forgotten.

It was beginning to be quite noticeable – even to me – how much my father had deteriorated, and for the first time I realised that his prolonged illness had developed into something a little more serious than a sore throat. He seldom ventured out of doors, and, had there been an abundance of nourishing food, he would have been unable to swallow it. But he had retained his gentle disposition, which says much for a man who must have suffered great mental anguish.

He talked to me long and often about my future, but there were times when his continued use of such phrases as 'I would like' or 'be sure to do' arose in me a horrible feeling that something was terribly amiss.

The blow fell one afternoon in January 1923.

Dad had visited the chest hospital for his monthly routine check-up and when he arrived back home there was nothing in his face to suggest anything out of the ordinary.

He must have been quite unaware that I was sitting on the settee when he drew from his pocket a slip of paper. He handed it to Mother and said very quietly, 'That is my death warrant.'

I sat up, open-mouthed, and looked at him as he buried his face in his hands. By the inflection of his voice I knew he was quite serious.

Mother hurriedly hustled me outside and I ran swiftly to see Fred. I was in tears when I told him what Dad had said.

I was astonished when, white-faced, he said to me, 'Dad has known for some months, so has Mother and so have I that there was no cure for his throat.'

I gasped, 'Do you mean he's dying?'

Fred just nodded.

There is no way I can adequately describe my feelings as I stood there crying, listening to the comforting words of Fred.

Due mostly to my age, everything had been hidden from me, but the stark way in which I had learned the truth made me wish I had been told earlier how ill Dad really was.

I returned home with Fred some time later to find that Dad was resting, and a tearful Mother was waiting to tell us that he was to be admitted to Walkergate Hospital the following day.

Hearing such news finally convinced me that he was doomed to die – perhaps very soon – because only those patients whose condition was hopeless were admitted to that dreaded hospital.

We were all in the kitchen the following day when the ambulance arrived, but Dad, still as independent as ever, refused the offer of a stretcher with a wry comment, 'I will be carried out of this house only once.'

And so, choked with grief, I watched that very brave man, with only a blanket around his shoulders, walk unaided to the ambulance.

That unhappy day was to end on a cruel note, caused mainly by an insolent and churlish remark passed by mother's sister, Aunt Bella.

I was well aware that she didn't much care for me; however, shortly after the ambulance had departed (Mother had gone too), Bella looked at me and then snarled, 'You can't go to college now you snotty young bugger – you will have to get a job.' But she certainly had not anticipated Fred's violent reaction. Hopping on one leg, he grabbed her and almost threw her to the ground, at the same time saying, 'Mind your own bloody business!'

What we didn't realise at that moment was just how far reaching the words of that unpleasant aunt were.

Chapter Thirty-Four

So much had happened since Dad had been taken to hospital – to slowly die. Home life had become an absolute shambles, with Mother understandably preoccupied with his illness and unable to apply herself to the simplest of household chores.

Her sister Bella had been given explicit instructions (by Fred) not to interfere in any way, so it was left to him and I to keep the home going and attend to the needs of the two youg'uns. (Fred was a tower of strength during that traumatic period, despite his broken leg.)

I had given very little thought to my impending entry to grammar school – which would have been in the January of that year – even though a voucher had been received from the authorities which would have enabled me to purchase everything I needed. But as with many other matters, Mother had either forgotten or couldn't be bothered to deal with it.

Deep down, however, I was becoming aware, with some sadness, that I would never achieve my Father's ambitious hopes for me. Why was I so sure? Well. The week before I was due to register at the school, I came face-to-face with the true state of our circumstances – there was no money (as soon as Dad had been admitted to hospital his relief was stopped) and no food in the house. I made that discovery one morning when I looked in the larder and found it empty. As I gazed at the bare shelves, Mother said, 'Go up to Mack's (the tick shop) and get a loaf, some margarine and tea. Tell him I will pay at the weekend.'

So there it was. How could I possibly go to High School when there was no food in the house? There was only one thing to do – forget High School and get a job.

Fred, who was sorely troubled by his inability to work, was furious when I told him of my intention. 'Dad will never let you do that,' he argued, but we both knew that he would not be around long enough to know.

We also knew that Mother needed assistance, and the only person we could think of to help was Granddad Henderson, who had not visited us since the spud-throwing incident. He lived in Heaton, so I hurried there one evening, not knowing what to expect. He was horrified to learn of Dad's condition and hot-footed it back with me. I left him and Mother alone and went round to Fred's place.

Later, we went home to find Granddad alone (he had given Mother money to go shopping), and, after expressing his concern, he began discussing my future.

'You realise that going to college is now out of the question,' he began. Odd though it was, I resented him telling me that, despite the fact I had made up my own mind to find work. Had he expressed a few words of regret I may not have felt so hurt, but he didn't. I made no comment.

In time I soon found that suitable employment wasn't easy to find. There were plenty of vacancies for errand boys, but the average wage was six shillings for a six-day week.

The solution was provided by my friend Bob, who had decided to join the Navy, but, having to wait almost a year before he was old enough to be accepted, he had to find a temporary job. He found it down a coalmine. He told me, 'There is no point in my doing anything else but a labourer's job until I join up, so I might as well work in a mine where I get an average wage of twenty-five shillings a week.' It was the wage that swung it for me.

My career in the mines was of comparatively short duration, but during that time I was to experience the full gamut of emotional and physical pain. I was to learn how vast the chasm between college boy and pit-boy, but I also became aware of a toughness and resilience blossoming within me – traits I would come to rely on in the years ahead.

I began my first shift at Hazelrigg Colliery on the early shift, which was from 4 a.m. until noon. As the pit was about six miles from Newcastle, it was necessary to leave home at 1.30 a.m.

I was fortunate to have Bob on the same shift because he knew the ropes. We walked up the North Road to Gosforth and there we turned off the main road and walked towards a rail-siding, where our train was standing. We had gone only a few steps when the engine gave a couple of warning toots and Bob shouted, 'We had better hurry!'

He set off at a trot along the track and I followed, sliding all over the place in the stiff new boots Mother had managed to buy for me. Suddenly, I tripped over one of the sleepers and went headlong into a signal gantry. Bob helped me up and we scrambled to the train, which we boarded just as it was setting off. I could feel blood running down my face but had to wait until we had alighted in the pit yard before Bob could see what the damage was. 'I think your nose is split, better call at the ambulance room.'

The attendant cleaned my face and assured me that the cut was only slight. Then he asked, 'What is you name?' I told him. 'What's your tally number?' 'I haven't got one. I'm a new starter.' He looked at me for a few moments then turned to his mate. 'Here's a lad having first aid and he hasn't even started in the fuckin' pit!'

I made my way home with Bob after that first shift, feeling very sore and very tired. Not surprising really, considering that after bashing my face, I had been dropped at a terrifying speed down into the bowels of the earth, and that in turn had been followed by seven hours of non-stop work at the shaft bottom.

The working area resembled an underground railway station with two sets of tracks, one for full tubs and the other for the empties. They were coupled in sets of twenties and at regular intervals the empty ones would be whisked away into a black tunnel. Shortly afterwards, a set of full ones would come hurtling out of the tunnel, which were then uncoupled and sent to the surface. For seven hours I coupled, uncoupled, coupled, uncoupled – skinning my knees and jamming my fingers. I was yelled at, cursed at, and even laughed at thanks to my bumbling efforts to keep the tubs moving. The heavy pit boots began to skin my ankles and weighed a ton.

I was thankful that afternoon to board the train back home – I was knackered!

Fred blew his top when he saw the state I was in, but I was much too tired to argue. I quickly bathed in the old tin bath and tottered to my bed. I was asleep within seconds.

I was awakened by the sound of voices. My face was throbbing, and, when I tried to turn over, I groaned aloud because my whole body was aching. I lay there, berating myself for taking a job down a pit, and wondering why I hadn't had the sense to take an errand boy's job, regardless of pay. Then I remembered that Mother was receiving only a food voucher from the parish and what we needed was some hard cash.

The door opened and Mother entered with the unwelcome news that it was eleven o'clock. I dressed and made my weary way into the kitchen.

'Dear me, what a mess your face is in!' said Mother. I looked in the mirror and was confronted with a shocking reflection. My nose was twice its normal size, I had a peach of a black eye, and my lug-holes were black with coal dust – the result of a hasty bath.

Mother began washing my face. 'How do you like your job?'

'Like it? Look at my face!'

'You'll feel better tomorrow.'

'There will not be a tomorrow!'

'What do you mean?'

'I am not going back.'

'You know I have no money?'

'Yes.'

'And that Fred won't be able to work for at least another two months?'

'I know that too.'

'And the bairn's clothes are threadbare?'

Because I was suffering from the effects of a bad first day at the pit, I failed to see that she was begging for my help. She brushed her face wearily and it was then that I saw the tears in her eyes.

I was filled with remorse as I realised how sorely troubled she was. There was Dad's illness and an acute shortage, not only of money, but of food and clothes as well. I knew then that I would return to the pit, because without some kind of steady income, our family could not survive.

I was still sore and weary as I trudged up the North Road the following day, but most of my ill-temper had been replaced by a sense of urgency.

Chapter Thirty-Five

My second day at the pit may not have started as painfully as the first, but it was equally as miserable. There had been a steady fall of rain that morning and Bob and I were soaked by the time we boarded the train at Gosforth. Like the rest of the lads, I was shivering when I entered the cage for the stomach-raising drop.

I duly presented myself to the overman, a tall man with enormous hairy eyebrows. 'Right,' he bawled, 'go to the stables, collect a pony, and report back to me.'

I turned away from him but as I did so my lamp rapped against a tub, and promptly went out.

The big man looked at me. 'What's your name?' he asked. I told him. 'You are from Newcastle then?' I nodded. He sighed deeply and patted me gently on the back. 'Never mind, son,' he said, 'all you townies are the same – FUCKIN' USELESS!' He yelled the last two words in my face.

I was in no mood for that kind of abuse, and had it not been for Bob (who was standing behind me), my mining career would have ended there and then. He led me to the stables, where I collected a spare lamp and a wicked looking pony.

'Right,' yelled the overman, 'go with those lads over there.' He pointed to a group of men and boys. When I joined them, one of the men asked, 'Ist thou wor new marra?'

'Am thor new marra,' I replied politely.

'Howway thin, let's git thi fuckin' lang wark owwer,' he said. With that he and the others made their way to the black tunnel and joined the long procession of men making their way in.

'A lang wark,' the man had said. Jesus, we walked and walked and walked, ever deeper into the earth. There was plenty of headroom, but by God it was hot! I had a king-sized thirst, my arms were aching from hanging on to the pony, and I was sweating like the proverbial pig.

The group I was with eventually turned off the main tunnel and proceeded along another slightly narrower one. I discovered that the roof was also much lower when a lump of skin was peeled off my head by an overhead beam. When I yelped a man behind me said, 'Thou hast ti keep thi heed doon marra!' I massaged the pigeon's egg and walked on. After what seemed like hours we reached what was called a landing; it was a gallery similar to that at the shaft bottom, but on a smaller scale. 'This is where you work,' said one of the lads.

He explained everything to me. His job was to connect the full tubs to the hauling cable and they would then be hauled to the shaft bottom and a set of empties would then be returned.

My job was to hitch the pony to two or three empty tubs and drive them to a smaller landing about half a mile further in-bye, where I would collect full ones from a 'putter' (a man who hauled them from the coalface) and bring them back to the landing stage. Incidentally, the poor pony had to carry the heavy shafts around, which were U-shaped, and they were connected to the tub by a pin fixed to the bottom of the 'U'.

My mate accompanied me on my first trip in-bye and it was quite uneventful – apart from knocking further lumps of skin off my cranium. But there were times while waiting for the putter when I became a little unnerved by the unnatural silence, which was broken occasionally by the creaking of the supports and rumblings from the roof. I had visions of millions of tons of rock falling and entombing me. Help!

Time passed quickly that day, and I was agreeably surprised when my mate said, 'Make this your last journey.' He watched while I hitched the shafts on to the tub, then said 'Try sitting on the shafts this time, it will be easier for you and the pony knows the way.' He showed me how to sit on the end of the shafts, which was between the tub and the pony's arse.

I had travelled about half the journey – thinking how much easier it really was – when the pony suddenly lifted its tail. OK, perhaps I should have anticipated what was going to happen, but I was a greenhorn, wasn't I? Now, I imagine that few of you will have experienced the doubtful pleasure of having a dirty-mannered pony fart in your lug-hole. Ugh! I almost choked to death! But that was only the prelude.

Perhaps I should explain that the tunnel along which I was travelling was only a little wider than the width of the tubs, therefore it wasn't possible, or safe, to jump off the shafts unless the pony was at a standstill. So there I sat, helpless, while a veritable avalanche of scalding hot horse shit cascaded into my lap! So ludicrous was the situation that I burst into hysterical laughter, and so intense was it that I ended up sobbing. It was as though a safety valve had been released and all my pent up emotions came flooding out at that moment. I think my whole outlook on life changed at that moment; certainly I had left my boyhood behind me.

Four weeks passed – a period during which I learned to take the rough with the rough (there was no smooth). I no longer blistered my fingers or scraped my knees, and avoiding the low beams had become second nature. But most importantly, I had settled to the role and accepted it – at least for the time being.

Although after just four weeks there was no discernable improvement in our home life, Mother was, however, looking a little less apprehensive. To help prevent her from brooding, the doctor advised her to find part-time work, and so she carried on with her charring.

It cannot be denied that Dad's illness and the knowledge that he was dying began to affect us deeply. Only Mother was allowed to visit him, and it became more and more distressing to learn after each visit that his condition was worsening.

One lamentable aspect of his illness was the 'couldn't-care-less' attitude of his relatives. Quite properly, Mother had informed them of the crisis, but they made no response, until one Sunday morning, when to our complete surprise, Dad's brother john came to the house.

His distaste for our spartan surroundings was obvious, and after asking a few questions about Dad he beat a hasty retreat, leaving behind a small jar of calf's foot jelly – 'for Sam,' he said. How this would help a dying man defied adequate comment. We no longer wondered why Dad had washed his hands of them.

Our hopes for a miracle were dashed two weeks later, when Mother returned from a visit to the hospital. She was distressed but calm when she told us that nothing more could be done and that Dad had expressed a wish to come home. He wanted to be with his family.

It was a difficult decision for Mother to have to make. She had been advised by the doctors that there was the danger of infection, and in view of that they suggested he should remain in hospital. But, like us, she dearly wanted him home, and it was Fred who finally settled the matter.

'Dad wants to come home, so we will have him home,' he declared. 'I will sort things out here.' Dear old Fred – he certainly did. Within hours the kitchen had been cleared and a single bed installed. Arrangements had been made for young Jim and Dora to sleep with a neighbour, and I would sleep with my pals – the Peters brothers.

Dad was brought home two days later when I was on an early shift at the pit. On my return, Mrs Peters told me that Dad was very restless and it would be better if I didn't go and see him until he had settled down a little. I had a talk with Fred and he agreed that I should wait until the next day.

When Bob and I left for the pit the following morning, I saw the dim light through the window of our kitchen, and I had a feeling that I ought to go in and see Dad – so I did. Fred was sitting with Mother and her sister. I walked to the bedside and was delighted when he turned his head and gave me a kind of half smile. But my pleasure was soured when I saw that the father I loved was now a shell, gasping for breath through a tube protruding from his throat.

When I took his hand he tried to say something, but the words wouldn't come. He motioned impatiently to Mother, who gave him a pencil and paper, then very laboriously wrote something and handed it the paper to me. Squeezing back the tears, I managed to read the faint writing: 'Keep your head down son,' it said. I wasn't able to speak, so I nodded and again he smiled. Then I left.

He died four hours later.

I am not going to dwell on those grievous days before the funeral, but I well remember seeing Dad's family standing a little distance from the grave, and Fred's angry comment, 'They must have a bloody conscience!' There were four other mourners, who we were pleased to see – those two good ladies and their husbands from Ashington.

Later, Fred and I stood in our kitchen waiting for the last of the mourners to finish eating (some of whom had to rely on a funeral to obtain an occasional feed!). 'It's up to you now youg'un,' he said. I could only nod.

Time can eradicate the pain of losing a loved one, but not the memory, and it was a long time before I ceased to expect Dad to walk in every time the door opened. With little more than my wages coming in, we were once again giving the corned beef a right old hiding. Mother, suffering from a nervous breakdown, had to give up her cleaning job, and two months were to pass before Fred was given the all-clear. However, in time, Fred returned to work and Mother recovered so well that she resumed her charring.

As we neared the end of 1923, it dawned on me that I had been neglecting my confirmation classes, so when I found the opportunity, I visited the church and saw the vicar. He was very sympathetic and understood why I had been absent for so long. I agreed to resume classes because, inwardly, I knew it was what Dad would have wanted me to do.

★ ★ ★

I hadn't been aware that Bob was superstitious until one morning when we were boarding the train at Gosforth. I climbed into a carriage and took a seat, expecting him to follow me, but when he hadn't appeared as the engine gave its warning toot, I looked out of the window and saw that he was standing on the siding, searching feverishly through his pockets.

I yelled to him to get a move on, but after another apparently vain search he shouted, 'You go on, I'm going back home.'

'What's up?' I asked. He just shook his head and began walking back towards the North Road.

I could think of no reason for his strange conduct, and I pondered over it throughout my shift. In fact, I was so disturbed that I called at his home immediately after work.

Bob looked somewhat embarrassed when I asked him what had been the matter, then he fished in his pocket and brought out an object. 'This,' he said. 'I had forgotten it.'

'What is it?' I asked.

'It's a button from Dad's uniform – he gave it to me as a keepsafe before he went to France. Wherever I go, the button goes with me.'

I thought it odd at the time, but as I grew older I realised how touching it was for a boy to place so much faith in a brass button from his dead father's uniform.

★ ★ ★

Now I never knew how a particular conversation began one morning as Bob and I, and a few other lads, walked along the North Road. It was a lovely morning – for a change – but suddenly, in the midst of our animated chatter, we heard the mournful howling of a dog.

'That's a sign of death,' said one lad.

'It's probably a ghost come back as a dog,' said another.

Then there began a general discussion about ghosts, which was interspersed with such comments as, 'If you saw a ghost you would shite yourself.'

I had taken no part in the noisy discourse (it brought back the memory of Dad's encounter with the mysterious Thing), but as we approached the Blue House with the argument still raging, Bob tuned to a big-mouthed lad who had professed to not being scared of ghosts and said, 'If you were to see a ghost now, what would you do?'

Before the lad could answer, Bob pointed towards the open space of the moor. 'Why don't you go and see what that is?'

All eyes followed in the direction of Bob's pointing finger and a deathly hush came over the company. Not a hundred yards from us we saw a vision in white gliding over the grass.

'What the hell is it?' we whispered.

'It must be a ghost,' Bob whispered back.

'Fuck that, I'm off,' said big-mouth boy.

Most of the lads then scattered in all directions, leaving only three of us – but the reason we hadn't followed them was that we were too scared to move!

We continued to watch as the ghostly figure, with arms outstretched, slowly turned and began to glide towards us.

'Sod it, I am away,' said our third companion, and promptly bolted.

The hackles on my neck were sticking out like spears and my heart was pounding, but Bob and I remained motionless as the frightening vision drew nearer and nearer – then it halted. Then, after a short pause, it turned and moved off again, gliding along parallel to the road.

'Come on, let's follow it,' said Bob.

'You can bugger off,' I hissed back.

He then put his hand in his pocket and pulled out the brass button. 'Come on,' he said, 'We won't come to any harm while I have this in my hand.' Without waiting for my reaction, he started tiptoeing towards one of the entrances leading on to the moor like a would-be burglar.

It was the fear of being left alone that made me follow him, and when we reached the grass we saw that our friend had stopped once more and was only about thirty yards from us.

Once again my hair stood on end when the thing emitted a series of low moans and began making circular movements with its arms.

'Where's the bloody button?' I asked, through chattering teeth.

Bob suddenly grabbed my arm and I gave a startled yelp. 'Listen,' he whispered. 'What do you hear?' All I could hear at that moment was my teeth chattering!

But then I heard what sounded like sobbing, which was followed by an anguished voice saying, 'God help me, where am I?'

'Bugger me,' I said, 'It's a woman.' At that moment she turned and faced us, and when she saw us standing only a few yards away from her, she gave an ear-piercing scream and fell to the ground.

Suddenly I had a brainwave. 'Listen Bob,' I said, 'You stay here and I will run to the copper's house at Grandstand Road and knock him up.'

Bob agreed and I set off to the policeman's house, which wasn't far. On arrival I hammered on the door and, to my relief, it was opened almost immediately by the copper.

'There's a woman on the moor,' I gasped, 'And she is wearing only a nightdress.' To my surprise the policeman said, 'Well done lad. I have just been informed that a lady sleepwalker who lives in Claremont Road has been missing for more than two hours.'

Together, we hurried back to find Bob sitting beside the woman with his jacket around her shoulders. The poor woman was sobbing bitterly as the constable, after taking our names, picked her up and carried her to the small police station.

All's well that end's well, did you say. Hardly! We missed our bloody train and had to return home.

But we both received a nice letter from the woman's relatives, thanking us for our prompt action.

Yet I wonder, if it had really been a ghost, would Bob's brass button have kept us safe?

Chapter Thirty-Six

I was bored with the pit, tired of that long walk to Gosforth, and sick to death of arriving there soaked to the skin. There came a morning when the journey proved particularly foul; it had rained almost non-stop and had been accompanied by a freezing wind. In fact, Bob had been so disgusted, he decided to pack the job in at the end of the week.

To make matters worse, I had been moved from the dry district in which I had worked to another, where there was almost always at least six inches of water to splodge through. You can imagine my disgust when I arrived there that morning to find that the pumps were not working and the water was almost up to my knees.

It was a damned awkward place to work because the whole main roadway resembled a switchback railway, and some of the gradients were so steep that tubs had to be hauled up and lowered by mechanical means.

I was in a sour mood as I coupled up six empties and attached them to a hawser, which, in turn, was connected to a hauling machine at the top of the bank. I signalled the operator (by pulling a cord which was connected to a bell at the top) and the set of tubs moved off. It was quite a long haul, and when I saw the last tub disappear into the darkness I moved over to the other track, where my water bottle was hanging.

I was guzzling away when I heard a strange rumbling coming from the direction of the gradient. Thinking that a fall of stone might have occurred, I peered fearfully up the incline. Then, to my horror, I saw the empty set come hurtling out of the gloom!

I was frozen to the spot, petrified with fear. Before I could move or even think, the leading tub slewed off the rails and came for me – then, nothing.

I came round as I was being placed on a stretcher, then I was rushed to the shaft bottom where I passed out again. When I regained my senses, I found myself in the Infirmary, suffering from a dislocated shoulder, lacerations to the head, and severe bruising. I was detained overnight, but I did receive a visit from a naturally panic-stricken Mother.

Thinking back on the incident, I realised just how lucky I had been. Had I not crossed to the other track for a drink of water then I would have been on the same track as the runaways, and with no room to move, I would doubtless have been badly injured, if not killed. (Bob thought so too, and promptly packed the job in there and then!)

Fred blew his top when he saw the state I was in, and upset Mother when he said, 'Had he been at college it would not have happened.'

It took about four weeks for my shoulder to heal. I was firmly resolved not to return to the pit – my frightening experience had made any thought of going back terrifying. So when Terry offered me hope of employment with his firm I jumped at it, even though the wage was only 7/6 per week. Mother was aware of my determination not to return to Hazelrigg, and so any objections she may have had would have been pointless – but she made none.

Two days before I was due to see Terry's boss, poor Fred arrived home almost in tears – he had been paid off. It meant that, until he got another job, we would soon be

back to the straitened circumstances that had been our lot
for so long. Fred felt so badly about it that he even considered getting a job at the pit, but such a course would
have been suicidal for him in view of his chest.

So, once again, I set off on that miserable walk up
the North Road, and how I missed the company of my
friend Bob! I returned to Hazelrigg with a heavy heart.
No one would have minded had I taken a job with Terry,
but 7/6 would have been a poor substitute for twenty-
five bob.

There were, however, some lighter moments. Pride of
place must go to Fred who, a little sheepishly I thought,
imparted some startling news.

'I'm courting,' he said.

'You're what?'

'I'm courting, and no wisecracks!'

'You're not old enough.'

'I'm nearly eighteen,' he said, huffily.

'I said nothing for a few moments because I realised
how quickly the years were passing. Just fancy, Fred
nearly eighteen and courting!

'Who is she?' I asked.

'You know her – Jack's sister, Margaret.'

'Does Ma know?'

'Nothing to do with her!'

'Oh.'

★ ★ ★

I went to the Palace Theatre with Terry that evening and
I noticed he was very quiet both going and coming back.
Now that was very unusual for him and I wondered if he
was sick or something.

'What's up with you tonight?' I asked.

'Nowt.'

'Nowt?'

'Nowt!'

We proceeded on our way, then suddenly Terry coughed and out of the side of his mouth he whispered, 'Am stuck on a tart.'

I nearly fell off the pavement.

'You're what?'

'She's a smasher,' Terry replied dreamily.

'Who is she?'

'Hilda,'

'Hilda who?'

'Hilda Smith,' he replied, smiling like a fool.

I looked at him closely. Here was a new Terry. Gone was the lovable rogue of yesteryear – the lad walking beside me was a smartly dressed eighteen year old in the throes of love. I swear had he flapped his arms he would have taken off!

I wanted to learn more about the girl who had the power to turn my tough friend into a love-struck jellybag.

'Where does she live,' I asked.

'Elswick Row, she works for the boss.'

'Have you told her?'

'I'm taking her out on Monday.'

So there it was – what a bloody turn up!

I reached a significant milestone of my own just prior to Christmas 1923, when I was presented to the Bishop of Newcastle and duly confirmed in St Matthew's Church.

As far as that particular Christmas is concerned, it was a very quiet affair for us – Dad's death was still in our minds. In any case, we had little to spare for anything but the bare necessities, because Fred's chest condition was making it difficult for him to obtain suitable employment and Mother had been unfortunate enough to suffer a bad dose of food poisoning, which had prevented her from working for almost two months.

During that period I couldn't expect my usual pocket money, but I was happy enough if I had a good supply of books to read.

I had come to accept, with a little pride, that I was the breadwinner, the mainstay, and it gratifies me even now to think I was able to shoulder the responsibilities of keeping the home going (and I say that in all humility).

But back to our love-struck Terry.

It must have been all of six weeks before he called to see me again, and I was alone in the house on a Saturday morning when he did.

'Hello stranger,' I greeted him.

'Fancy going to the Palace tonight?' he asked.

'No.' I replied.

'Why not?'

'You know why not.'

'I'll pay for you.'

'No, thank you.'

'Just thought I'd ask.'

'Thanks!'

Curiosity then got the better of me.

'What's up with that girl of yours?' I asked.

No answer, just a shrug.

'Packed her in, have you?'

'She packed me in.'

'Oh!'

There was a long pause, then Terry laughed.

'She has a lovely arse, but it was as cold as a boody poe!'

I had to ask. 'How the hell do you know?'

'Because I had my bloody hand on it!' he chortled.

I joined in the laughter – my friend was back to his usual self.

And if you're wondering, boody is a local term for ceramic!

Chapter Thirty-Seven

Once again I asked myself, 'What the hell am I doing here?' I had been moved to another pit district, one that had the dubious name of Slaughter Alley.

It was so-called because it had a notoriously unstable roof and falls occurred with frightening regularity, many of which had caused fatal accidents. There was green slimy water everywhere and the pervading smell of decay was ever-present in one's nostrils.

I hadn't really shook off the effects of that terrifying experience with the runaway tubs, and having to work in such conditions did little to raise my morale. In plain words, I was scared stiff!

But what was I to do? Because of the acute Depression, and the reluctance of the parish to issue cash to under-sixteens, workhouse tickets were being lobbed out to many unfortunate youths, an ignominy I was not prepared to accept under any circumstances.

My peace of mind was further shattered by a tragedy that occurred a few weeks after I had returned following my accident. Having been deprived of Bob's company, I began walking to the pit each morning with a lad named John who lived in the next street.

He was waiting for me at our usual meeting place on this particular morning, but he was not dressed for work. 'Dad's very ill,' he told me, 'And I am having a day off to help my mother.' I promised to inform his boss and set off alone.

I was proceeding along Percy Street when I heard the sound of running footsteps, and when I looked round I saw, to my surprise, that it was John. 'Mother says she can manage, and in any case I don't want to lose a day's pay,' he explained.

Just two hours after descending, poor John was crushed to death. He died for the sake of five bloody shillings!

I arrived back home after eight that morning, and a nasty scene developed almost immediately.

'A lad has been killed,' I told Mother.

'How awful!'

'I'm packing it in at the end of the week.'

'That wouldn't be wise.'

'What do you mean?'

'You know what happens if you cannot get work.'

'What?'

'I won't be able to feed and clothe you.'

I looked at her in amazement.

'Do you want me to spend my life down a mine?'

'No, but…'

'If you can't feed me then I will join the Navy.'

'I won't allow you to do that!'

'Why not?' I yelled.

'Because I need you at home.'

So the argument raged until, almost choked with frustration, I went to see Fred. At least he would listen!

'Try and stick it a little longer,' he said, to my surprise.

'Why the hell should I?'

'Has it ever occurred to you that Mother may marry again?'

'Eh?'

'She isn't an old woman you know, and if she should decide to re-marry then your problems will be solved.'

He concluded, 'I know how you feel, but try and stick it, at least for a few more weeks.'

If I have to explain why I had become so belligerent then the answer is simply fear! I had become terrified of working underground, and the shocking death of one of my mates had done little to allay that feeling. But I agreed to do what Fred had suggested.

There having been no major falls of stone in Slaughter Alley for more than a couple of weeks, I slowly began to lose the dread I had of the place, and that was as well, because I was spending most of my time peering nervously up at the roof, wondering if it was going to fall on me! But that treacherous roof had simply been lulling everyone into a false sense of security.

It happened the week after Easter, when I was on the afternoon shift. As I reached the bottom I was stopped by the overman, who asked me, 'Where were you working yesterday?' I was surprised by the question, because it was he who had sent me to the Slaughter in the first place, but I answered him. Then he told me something that turned my knees to jelly.

'Fifteen minutes after your shift left the area, the whole fuckin' roof caved in and we couldn't trace you. Where had you got to?' I tried to gather my thoughts, then I remembered. 'My pony went lame and the deputy sent me off early to walk it slowly to the stables.' The overman shook his head. 'Then you can thank a lame pony for probably saving your life.'

I was sent to another district the following day, one in which falls were rare and there was a total absence of water.

I had to do the same kind of job – taking empty tubs in-bye and returning with full ones. I was by then quite an expert at riding on the shafts, but I always kept a wary eye on the pony's tail!

After three or four days of comparatively peaceful shifts, my fears had begun to abate, and as I hitched my pony up for another trip in-bye I was actually singing.

When I reached the inner landing I saw that there were four full tubs, and, although the maximum load a pony was allowed to pull was three, I decided to haul the four because it was my last trip in-bye.

Giving the pony a slight tickle with my whip I set off, but then, for some unknown reason, the nag began to trot – which is against regulations. I tried to pull him up but he wouldn't have it, so I had to let him carry on trotting. I had hoped that the weight of the four full tubs (two tons) would slow him down – but not he!

I was just about to jump off when I heard an almighty 'crack' above my head, followed by a familiar rumble – a fall! The pony had made no effort to slow down and there was damn all I could do to stop him, but when he eventually did, it was with catastrophic suddenness.

Accidents are hard to describe afterwards and this one was no exception. I remembered the pony falling to his knees and the momentum of the four tubs turning him right over, and I was in the middle of it all. I well remembered the yell I gave when I felt an excruciating pain in my left leg; then I was hit on the head by something and knocked unconscious.

When I came to, I found that my lamp had gone out and, except for the faint glow of a spare one pinned to a prop about fifty yards away, I was in total darkness. My leg was trapped between the pony – which was lying motionless – and one side of the shaft. Somehow, I managed to free myself and crawl to the spare lamp, where I saw that blood was pouring from my leg. I also knew that my head was bleeding. I had to get to the outer landing, where I knew there would be a deputy, before I could receive treatment, so I set off at a crawl.

Fortunately, there was a deputy and after some hurried first aid, I was shunted to the shaft bottom – again!

A hairline fracture of the left leg, which was also badly lacerated, a gash on my head and multiple bruises to other parts of my body. Those were the injuries I was found to have when I was admitted to the Infirmary – for the fourth time in my life.

Once again I was detained overnight and arrived back home the following afternoon swathed in bandages and painted all over with iodine. Who said I was accident prone?

'This,' I said to Mother, 'Is the finish!' She didn't argue.

During the time it took my injuries to heal, I thought long and hard about my future and the events of the previous twelve months. I have to admit that no matter how hard I tried to convince myself, I no longer cared about higher education; I knew I would always regret the lost opportunity.

What then was in store for me? With a shudder I realised how easy it would be to become slowly but inexorably sucked into the vortex of struggling humanity that whirled around me.

My family had been in desperate straits many times leading up to that period, and it didn't seem humanly possible for us to sink any lower – but never was an assumption proved to be more wrong.

If anything, the employment situation had grown even worse. There was literally nothing available, and those who were fortunate to have jobs guarded them carefully, even to the extent of accepting a cut in wages. Not one of my pals had been able to find work, which was why Joe, Bob and Peter had joined the Navy.

Mother had managed to scrape along for a couple of weeks after my leg had healed, but eventually she had to apply to the parish for a food voucher.

I went with her and listened while she explained the reasons for the application to a man who eyed us with undisguised distaste. 'Take a seat,' he said, after finishing his third-degree examination.

Eventually we were ushered into an inner office, where we stood facing a man whose face resembled an over-pickled bloater! He cleared his throat with an exaggerated 'Hurrumph' and, without looking at us, said, 'We are allowing some assistance for yourself and the younger children, but we can do nothing for this idle young man, apart from admitting him to a workhouse.'

'No thank you,' said Mother, 'he is going to join the Navy.'

We had been back home only a few minutes when she said, 'You can forget about the Navy.'

'Why?'

'I can't let you go.'

Justified she might have been, but I was absolutely boiling with rage, and even though I was only fifteen and a half years old, I forgot she was my mother when my temper exploded.

'Do you realise,' I began, 'that I was denied a better education, that in order to help you I trudged up the North Road in all weathers for more than a year and then did a shift underground in inches of water. I have suffered two accidents, one of which almost killed me. I handed you my wages every week, and is it not true that my clothes consist of a second-hand suit, a pair of shabby boots and a patched-up shirt? And what do I get in return? The threat of the workhouse. And now you are denying me the opportunity of leaving this rat-infested cesspool.'

Mother remained silent. I was trembling and perhaps a little ashamed, but nothing would have made me apologise at that moment. I finished by saying, 'I am no longer a small boy, and if you continue to treat me as one then I will run away from home.' I dashed out of the house before she could answer.

For hours I walked aimlessly around the town, gazing enviously at the more affluent populace with their heavily-laden shopping bags, and there was I, a candidate for the bloody workhouse.

I made my way back home but I decided to call and see Fred first. I met him as I was going down Rye Hill – he was looking for me.

'Have you left home for good?' I asked, brusquely. He was a little taken aback but he answered truthfully. 'I soon will have.'

I could only nod my head because I was so dispirited.

'Mother has been looking for you everywhere; you've been missing for nearly six hours.'

'Did she tell you I had been offered a ticket for the workhouse?'

'No.'

'Did she tell you she will not let me join the Navy?'

'Yes she did, but—'

'Listen Fred, no buts; I am bloody fed-up. Look at me – after nearly a year's hard work I haven't a decent suit to wear!'

'Granddad's at home and he wants to talk to you.'

'Right, but you had better come with me because I am not going to put up with this much longer.'

Surprise number one greeted us when we got home – Mother and the two kids were tucking into bacon and eggs.

Mother didn't mention my absence, but when she got up to cook a meal for Fred and I she said, 'I would like you to listen carefully to what your Granddad has to say.'

'I can get you a job,' he began.

'Oh, can you?'

'Yes, if you want it.'

'Where?' I asked.

'Down Elswick Colliery.'

I jumped as though I had been stabbed in the backside, 'No!' I yelled, 'No, No!'

'Wait a minute,' Granddad said.

I had heard it all before: the slump, the difficulties following Dad's death, Fred's accident, the rent in arrears, money owing to the tick shop; and so he went on. But I shook my head and said firmly, 'No!'

But Granddad was not only patient but crafty with it. 'Look,' he continued, 'I am going to clear your mother's debts and give her enough money to last a couple of weeks. I am also prepared to buy you a new rig-out, but only on condition that you take this job.' I carried on eating my eggs and bacon.

Then he added, 'An awful lot of lads have applied for this job, but I have pulled a few strings and got it for you. It is only a small pit, it is quite dry and it is only ten minutes' walk from here. Now then, what about it?'

I knew I was being backed into a corner and it annoyed me a little. I snapped at Fred, 'What would you do?'

'You must make up your own mind up,' he replied quietly.

Mother hadn't said a word but I could sense her anxiety, so with a sigh I said, 'Right, I'll take it, but only until I'm sixteen.'

Granddad kept his promise, and I duly descended Elswick Colliery early one morning in the merry month of May 1924.

But my conscience troubled me. I realised I had been wrong to shout at Mother; after all, she was not to blame for our circumstances.

The truth was, I was wallowing so much in my own misfortune that I had become blind to the difficulties Mother was facing, and I failed to see how frail Fred was with his bad chest. I had to admit that my dented pride had warped my sense of fairness and turned me into a selfish young bastard.

But I did benefit from that particular self-analysis, and I am sure my family forgave me.

Chapter Thirty-Eight

Granddad was telling the truth on two accounts regarding Elswick; it was a dry pit and it was only a ten-minute walk. But the deceitful old goat hadn't told me that the workings were as hot as Hades and only three feet high! The methods of working and the general layout were similar to those at Hazelrigg, but there was one big difference – there were no ponies, which meant that all tubs had to be manhandled.

Having had some experience of working underground, it was not necessary for me to be acclimatised at the shaft bottom (the normal procedure for new starters), so I was sent in-bye right away. Some two miles later I reported to a deputy, who looked me over and said, 'You look a strong lad, go with that chap over there and he will show you the ropes.'

I approached a lad of about my age who was stripped to the waist, so I did the likewise. 'We work in there,' he said, pointing to one of the side roads that branched off the main landing. He uncoupled an empty tub and began pushing it into the entrance of the road, and I followed suit.

Now, the roof at the beginning of that road was at least five feet high, and because there is nothing difficult about pushing an empty, I felt reasonably happy. But I had gone only a few yards when my head hit the roof with a painful 'clunk', and, looking up, I was shocked to see that the ceiling was just a trifle higher than the tub!

Keeping my head well down I continued pushing, but then I yelled in agony when I felt a strip of skin being ripped off the bottom of my back – my arse was too high! I lowered it, but how was I to push a flaming tub when I was on my hunkers? I tried pushing with my head against the tub, but each time I put a foot forward my rump would come into contact with the roof, and off would come another strip of skin! In despair I stretched my legs out behind me, that didn't work either, I fell on my bloody belly!

However, after many more grunts and yelps I finally reached my destination – a small inner landing – to find my mate crouched behind a full tub. 'Grab one of these,' he yelled, and off he scuttled on the return journey, looking for all the world like a bow-legged crab!

After only one journey I was a mass of aches and pains, but with a sigh I placed myself behind a full tub and gave it a good, hard push – that was a mistake. I wasn't aware there was a down gradient on the return journey until the tub shot away and pulled me down onto my knees.

I got on to my hunkers and tried to hold it back, but my arse bumped against the sleepers, and if I raised my body, my head hit the roof! After several futile attempts, I realised I couldn't hold on much longer. I had been dragged on my belly for about half the journey when my cramped hands lost their grip, and I lay on the ground watching that damned tub disappearing further and further away.

Galloping like a chimpanzee I hurried after it, but it was hopeless. The blooming tub whizzed out of the darkness and on to the landing – and almost gave the deputy a heart attack!

'What the hell are you trying to do?' he yelled, when I made a sheepish appearance. 'Sorry, but it is my first go at it,' I replied. 'Aye, and it will be your fuckin' last!' he retorted angrily. Then he looked at me closely. 'Are you

Jack's grandson?' he asked. 'Yes, I am,' I replied. 'I've been looking for you. I want you to work on this landing.'

I was still working on this landing when my sixteenth birthday came along.

I am going to digress for a while because, during that year, I was deeply affected by a personal tragedy.

You may well have wondered whether or not I had forsaken the church. The answer is no, even though my attendance since my confirmation had been extremely rare. I had begun to understand the cynical attitudes of downtrodden people towards religion, and whenever I was asked if it had been of any benefit to me, I had to answer truthfully, 'No, not materially.'

However, after a fairly lengthy absence, I made my way to the church one Monday evening, and I must say I was looking very smart in the new clothes Granddad had bought me. (Actually I was making a belated visit to choir practice to ascertain whether my voice was any good or not.)

As always I was warmly welcomed by the regulars, but I was quite surprised when the vicar asked me to augment the choir at a wedding, which was to take place the following Saturday, and could I attend on the Thursday for a rehearsal of the ceremony? Of course I could.

There were no problems at the rehearsal; I watched with interest as the bride and her maids did their stuff, but just before the end, the lad standing next to me poked me in the ribs. 'Is she smiling at you?' he asked. 'Is who smiling?' I asked in return. 'The maid with the coloured glasses on,' he whispered. I glanced casually at the maids, but the one wearing glasses was then talking to her companion. 'I don't know her, she must have been smiling at you,' I said.

Come the Saturday and without doubt a lot of money had been spent on the wedding, the church was a mass of flowers of all varieties. There were about a hundred guests seated, and with the ladies in their colourful dresses and the men in claw-hammer coats, it presented a scene the like of which I had never seen before.

I watched, fascinated, as the beautifully gowned bride and her maids slowly made their way up the aisle to the altar, at which point we sang the first hymn. I glanced idly round while the vicar was doing his stuff, when a sudden movement by one of the maids caught my eye – she was the girl wearing the glasses. I turned my head quickly and looked at the lad who had pointed her out on the Thursday – the damned oaf was preening himself and smiling back at her!

After the ceremony, we, the choir, were standing in the changing room, when the bride's father entered, and, after thanking us for our services, he invited us all to have a night out at the Theatre Royal on a date to be arranged. I was delighted because the Gilbert and Sullivan season was in full swing.

But there was yet another surprise to come. 'Which one of you is Sam Herbert?' asked a guest who had entered the room. I was pointed out to him, then he said, 'Will you come with me for a moment?'

I was a little puzzled but I followed him out of the room and, standing in the passage, was the maid with the glasses on! 'Here he is,' said the man and left us.

She was gazing at me intently and I began to blush like a callow schoolboy, then she asked, 'Don't you know me?' I looked closely at her then I shook my head.

'Shame on you, Sam,' she said reproachfully, but then she removed her glasses and I almost whooped with delight. After three years here was my school friend Irene, whom I thought I'd said goodbye to forever!

She was as pretty as a picture in her maids' dress and while I stood gawping at her she leaned forward and kissed me on the cheek, something she had often done when we were going to school.

She had very little time to talk with me, so she promised to meet me in the church the following morning.

It dawned on me as I watched her walk away that she had never really been far from my thoughts, but what pleased me most was her obvious delight at seeing me. I made my mind up at that moment not to lose touch with her again.

Irene attended the morning service and afterwards told me she was in Newcastle for the weekend and was staying with an aunt in Wingrove Road. I walked back with her and as we made our way up Rye Hill we talked of many things.

'You didn't go to grammar school then,' she said.

'No, I couldn't.'

'I was sorry to hear about your father.'

'We miss him.'

'You work in the mines, don't you?'

'How do you know so much about me?' I asked.

'I was here some weeks ago and I was talking to the vicar about you.'

'Oh, I see.'

'My mother died some months ago.'

'What?' I gasped.

'It was very sudden.'

The fact that she was now an orphan strengthened my resolve to keep in touch with her.

We had been walking very slowly but as we reached Elswick Road, I noticed that Irene seemed to have some difficulty with her breathing; when I mentioned it, she brushed it off as being caused by a severe cold she'd had the previous week, but I insisted we take a tram for the remainder of the journey.

As the tram rattled it's way up Westgate Road, I said to her, 'Irene, I missed you a lot and I don't want to lose touch with you again. So, would you mind if I were to write to you now and again?'

'Please do,' she replied, 'Perhaps we ought to have written to each other before.'

I learned from her that she was still living in Whitley Bay with another aunt but, following the death of her mother, she had decided not to go to college.

Before I left her at the door of her aunt's house, we made tentative arrangements for me to visit her when circumstances permitted and I was to wait for her to write to me first. I was as happy as could be as I made my way home.

But one week passed, then two, then three, and when the fourth week passed and still no letter, I had to face the truth – she wasn't going to keep her promise. I toyed with the idea of calling her aunt, but I decided against it.

Was I hurt? Of course I was! After all, she had been very dear to me for more than ten years and she wouldn't deliberately hurt anyone – so what had gone wrong?

I kept my disappointment to myself, although I had found it very hard not to confide in Fred, who was well aware that something was upsetting me.

Five weeks passed and I was beginning to forget the whole business when, out of the blue, I learned why Irene had not written.

I had gone to church early on the Sunday morning – it was my turn to light the altar candles – and I was in the vestry collecting them when the vicar looked in. Strangely, he didn't bellow his usual cheery 'Good morning Sam,' instead he said, 'Will you come to my study Sam, I want to talk with you.'

I followed him to his study and after a hesitant cough he said, 'It's about your friend Irene.'

'What about her?' I asked.

'I am afraid that you will not be seeing her again.'

'Oh, I know that,' I said.

'She's dead, Sam.'

There was no mistaking what he had said, and those four words, spoken with dreadful simplicity, made my blood freeze. I looked at him with a mix of horror and disbelief as he continued, 'She came with her aunt to see me just before the wedding, and I learned from her aunt that she was receiving treatment for a blood disorder. Unfortunately, it was more serious than that. She collapsed the week after the wedding and was taken to hospital. She died last week from leukaemia, an incurable disease.'

I was so numbed by the shock that I only heard snatches of what he was saying. I was thinking, Irene, my lovely pig-tailed school friend, dead. First my sister, then my father, and now Irene.

I mentioned earlier how my belief in the Church had been sorely tested at times, well, the death of Irene almost destroyed it. I did not sing in the choir that morning, or ever again, and regular worship from that moment came to an end.

I left the church and made my way slowly down Rye Hill, oblivious to everything around me. The words of the vicar were still ringing in my ears, 'She's dead, Sam.'

I had reached the lane leading to The Avenue and as I turned into it, I almost collided with Thug and his cronies. I walked past them but then I was tripped from behind and sent flying headlong onto the pavement. As I picked myself up, one of the louts ran towards me and tried to kick me in the stomach, but I managed to avoid him. Then he came for me again and I had no alternative but to flatten him – and that gave Thug the opportunity he had waited for all those years.

Before I go on I must say this. I was only sixteen and a half against Thug's eighteen, but I was healthy and strong and almost as tall as he. His philosophy was simple – having almost murdered me on a previous occasion, there was no reason why he shouldn't repeat the performance.

But I had something he lacked – a promise to exact retribution for that fearful beating all those years back.

Thug flung off his jacket and came for me. For a few moments I thought I was going to crumble from the barrage of punches, head-butts and kicks, but somehow

I remained on my feet, and in doing so my enemy must have been surprised, because he suddenly backed away.

I discarded my own jacket. Settling-up time between us had arrived, and no longer was I going to back away from the lout who had tormented and ridiculed me for more than a decade.

So, when he came for me a second time, I took a deep breath and waded in. I forgot the promise I had made to my father, I ignored the teachings of the Church, I just went for him with everything I had.

I was unaware that a crowd had gathered, that Billy had flattened one of Thug's brothers and that Terry had 'sorted out' two of the other louts.

To my delight, my hated enemy began to back away and I went for him with renewed vigour; after a few more minutes he held his hand up and said, 'Enough,' but I was having none of that. Even though he fell to his knees I had no intention of backing off, because I remembered only too well the injuries he had inflicted, not only on me, but numerous other defenceless victims.

At last, when I saw that he had really had enough I backed away, and as I did so I felt a stinging blow to my back. I turned to see Thug's mother wielding a thick leather belt, and had Fred and Jack not dragged me away, I would have gone for her too.

Mother was almost hysterical when we entered the house, which wasn't hard to understand because my face was in a right old mess. My eyes were swollen, my mouth was cut and blood was pouring from my nose.

I plonked myself wearily on to a chair and Fred began to sponge my face. While he was doing so Terry and Billy came in, grinning like two Cheshire cats. 'You have put his bait up this time,' said Terry, 'So now you have got him out of your hair.'

Pleased though I was at the outcome of the battle, I regretted having broken the promise I had made to my

Father, and I vowed that never again would I behave like a damned animal.

So ended an unforgettable Sunday – first the shocking news of Irene's death, then the street battle with Thug.

I lay in bed that night thinking back, not only on the events of that day, but also to what had happened during the days, weeks and months since Dad had died. And I felt ten years older.

Chapter Thirty-Nine

Mother was very apprehensive in the aftermath of the battle because, generally speaking, families such as Thug's usually vented their spleen on some other member of the victor's family. But Fred agreed with me when I told her that the jibes and taunts simply had to be stopped, even though the manner in which it had been carried out was degrading.

Painful though my bruises were, there was an equally sore point I had to discuss with Mother.

'I'm leaving Elswick next week,' I said to her.

'Why?'

'What do you mean "why?"'

'You've got a good steady job, haven't you?'

'Mother,' I said, 'I wanted to leave the pit when I was sixteen – I am more than that now.'

'Right, please yourself, but don't start grumbling when your clothes become shabby and you have no money.'

Her last observation made me think, because work was still difficult to obtain, but I wanted to get away from mining before it was too late.

I thought about it for a while, then I decided to compromise – I would remain at Elswick while I was looking for something else.

I was on the early shift the following week, which suited me because no one would be around to see the bruises on my face, and when I returned home it would be covered with coal dust.

It was midway through the Wednesday shift when Mr Buckley (the deputy overman and friend of Grandad Henderson's) came to the place in which I was working accompanied by a new boy. 'I want you to show this lad how to work this landing because I have another job for you.'

I met Mr Buckley at the end of the shift and he explained all. 'Your grandfather is a good friend of mine and I promised him I would look after you, that is why I am moving you to the shaft-bottom. You will be there permanently and the pay is much better.'

Now what the hell was I to do? There was no point in my taking a permanent job when I intended to leave as soon as I could, but on the other hand I couldn't refuse a man who was helping me in order to keep a promise. I agreed to take it but I didn't tell him I would soon be leaving.

I got a further surprise when I returned home and told Mother what had happened.

'I know all about it,' she replied.

'What do you mean, you know all about it?'

'Because I spoke to your grandfather and he agreed to speak to Mr Buckley and ask him to try and get you a better job.'

'You did that behind my back, so it means you want me to be a pit-yacker all my life,' I yelled furiously.

'No, but…'

'There will be no buts Mother, I will leave the pit as soon as I can.'

I started the new job the following day. As Mr Buckley had said, the job was a good one; the working area was at least fifteen feet high, steel sheets covered the floor and the whole area was lit by electric lights.

My job was a fairly simple one – uncoupling full tubs when they had been hauled out, and coupling up the empties for despatch in-bye. But there were times when I had to help in the loading and unloading of the cages.

The first week had been quite uneventful, and I had come to the conclusion that if I'd had no aspirations beyond mining then it was the kind of job I would have wanted. However, on the Monday of the second week I left home with my written notice in my pocket.

We had been working for about two hours when the onsetter (chargeman) said, 'Right Sam, let's have the cage emptied then we will have a break.'

I watched as the cage appeared, and as was the usual procedure when there was to be a break in coal drawing, the cage stopped with the lower deck level with the floor. (The idea was to unload the bottom deck first, then the middle one and finally the top, thus ensuring that the cage would rest on the shaft-bottom when idle.)

I grasped the top of the tub and pulled and at the same time the cage suddenly dropped. I felt a seering pain in my left hand – it had been trapped between the top of the tub – which was partially resting on the sheets – and a cross-bar on the cage. Then the cage lurched and I felt a horrible crunching in my hand. I passed out.

I learned later from Mr Buckley that had the cage made any further downward movement then my hand would have been sheered off. Fortunately, the engine-man up top had realised his mistake and corrected it immediately.

I was detained in the Infirmary (yet again) pending a decision whether or not to amputate my little finger, and to undergo an operation on the hand. Happily, it wasn't found necessary to chop off the digit.

I am sure you will agree that to suffer a dislocated shoulder, a fractured leg, and an almost shattered hand during my few years as a miner, together with the mental anguish that resulted, was ample justification for my desire to leave mining to those who were not quite as accident prone as I was.

Very little of interest happened during those idle months, except that Granddad called every Saturday morning and gave me half a crown. He was horrified to learn how close I had come to permanent disablement. I was only a little worse off financially because I was on full compensation, plus a generous payment from an accident fund, and as Mother was charring up to four days a week, it would be fair to say that our living standard was reasonable.

Neither Fred nor Terry were able to obtain employment, and I found their company most acceptable during my enforced idleness. Usually though I was content to read – which meant anything from books on basic English to the Bible.

One source of great pleasure to me was the musical box that had been so highly treasured by Dad. Time and again I would wind it up then listen raptly to the tinkling music of *The Gondoliers*. In fact, I played it so often that Mother began to be irritated by it.

'For heaven's sake give that damned thing a rest,' she bawled one evening, 'I am sick of hearing it.' Then why not buy a gramophone?' I suggested. To my astonishment, she agreed to do so! A few days later a gramophone and half a dozen records were duly delivered. (It is interesting to note that being the owner of one of those things was considered to be a sign of affluence, and many owners would 'swank' about it by poking the horn out of an open window and letting the music sally forth!)

Terry, Fred and I spent many happy hours listening to it, and because records were only three pence and six pence each, we soon had a good variety of them. (Terry's favourite was 'Bollicky Bill the Sailor'!)

I think we had owned the thing about three months when, on a Saturday morning, we pooled our resources in order to buy the latest hit. Off went Terry to the record shop and when he returned I was about to make the long trek to the netty, so he agreed to wait until I got back before playing it.

There was a queue waiting when I arrived and it must have been all of half an hour before my turn came, but I had just settled down (with a sigh of relief) when I heard Terry shouting at the top of his voice, 'Sammy, Sammy, where are you?'

'In here,' I yelled back. 'What the hell's up?'

'Better get a move on,' he screamed.

'What for?'

'A strange man has just arrived in your house!'

'What are you talking about? What strange man?' I shouted.

'He just walked in…'

'What do you mean "he just walked in"?' (I was losing my temper!)

'…and pinched the fuckin' gramophone!'

I couldn't believe my ears. A stranger had pinched the gramophone?

I dashed out of the netty to be confronted by an extremely agitated Terry. 'No kidding Sammy,' he burbled, 'A bloke just walked in and swiped the fuckin' thing!'

We galloped home and sure enough the gramophone had gone.

'Who was he?' I asked.

'Search me,' replied a mystified Terry.

'Did he say anything?'

'He said something about Newton's.'

Then the penny dropped – that was the name of the firm from whom Mother bought the gramophone. It had been reclaimed – perhaps for non-payment. Dealers didn't bother taking clients to court; they simply whipped the goods away. It wasn't unusual for some luckless non-payer to be tipped on to the floor and the bed they had just been lying on carried away!

My worst fears were confirmed when Mother returned home; she was really upset because the payment showed only one week's payment was owed – she had forgotten to call in the previous week.

Whatever the reason, the fact remained that the gramophone had been taken away in full view of the scandalmongers in The Avenue, who soon made their feelings known.

'I told you so!'

'Wouldn't pay a fuckin' shilling a week.'

'Snotty-nosed gits!'

And so on and so on.

The following week, Mother called at the dealer's, hoping that her explanation would persuade them to let us have the gramophone back. Lo and behold their account book showed that nothing had been paid for a whole two months. Someone had obviously been on the fiddle because Mother's payment card was proof enough and after many apologies the firm agreed to supply another gramophone – a new one!

Watching the new gramophone being delivered was food and drink to the scandalmongers.

'Get things and won't pay for them!'

'I hope the fuckin' spring breaks!'

And so on and so on.

Fred decided to retaliate in a most unexpected manner.

He called home the following Sunday morning at about seven o'clock with a record under his arm, and, although it was still dark and the neighbours would be snoring their heads off, he opened the window and poked the horn out.

We laughed as their sleep was rudely shattered by the stirring music of Colonel Bogey.

And the same to you!

Chapter Forty

Never were two brothers so different in mannerisms and dispositions as were my pals Bob and George. Bob, the younger of the two, was a rough and ready character who was never averse to joining in most of our scatter-brained escapades.

George, on the other hand, was diffident to a degree, but his most outstanding characteristic was his tightness with money. For example, it wasn't unusual for him to run from The Avenue to the Palace Theatre whilst we took a tram – just to save a penny! But there were times when he would cause some irritation by his reluctance to spend more than he had to.

The amusing incident I am leading up to began some months after Bob, Billy, Joe and Peter had joined the forces. Now that meant that there were only three of us – me, Terry and George – left, so we began to take it in turn to sit in each other's houses one night each week to play cards, ludo, or any other game.

It was agreed that each of us would buy a bottle of pop or ginger beer and swap drinks during the course of the evening.

However, George would roll up with a small bottle against our large ones, and, of course, ended up drinking a great deal more than he was paying for – and that didn't go down too well with Terry.

Yet he was to shake us to our very foundations by accomplishing the impossible – he began dating Alicia! Many lads (including myself) had tried to date her, but she was a haughty young miss and made no bones about expressing her opinion of the young males who tried their hand with her. So, how in the hell had our tight-fisted George managed it?

What shocked us most though was the cheerful manner in which he began to throw his money around. 'I only take a girl into the circle or the stalls,' he bragged.

Because George was spending most of his time with his lady-love, our usual dates in his house had almost come to an end, but there came a weekend when his mother had to visit a sick sister. As she had arranged to spend the weekend there, George had been obliged to look after his younger sister, and that meant he wouldn't be able to take Alicia out on the Saturday.

But he had a brainwave. 'Why don't we have a meeting in our house on Saturday evening,' he asked us. 'I will bring Alicia in to join us.'

Well, I wasn't too keen and I was sure Terry wouldn't relish the idea of watching the lovebirds gazing into each other's eyes all night, but to my astonishment he agreed. 'Good idea George, good idea!'

Terry and I duly called in on the Saturday with our usual large bottles; George, of course, had his usual small one.

Alicia was already there and we noticed she was looking none too happy – neither was George. Even Terry's cheerful banter failed to raise the slightest trace of a smile from either of them, and after an uncomfortable period of silence I asked, 'What's up with you two?' It was George who answered. 'She's disappointed because we cannot go to the pictures.'

At that moment Terry opened his bottle of Sasparilla and, in a casual tone, he said, 'Well, why don't you go? Sammy and I will give an eye on things here until you come back.'

I looked at him and had the feeling that he was up to skulduggery because he would not have normally agreed to babysit.

Alicia's face lit up. 'Go on,' Terry urged. 'Get yourselves away, you'll be back before nine.'

While he had been talking he had filled two glasses with bubbling pop. ' Here you are,' he said, 'Drink up and get yourselves away.'

Alicia sipped hers in an affected genteel manner, but George gulped his down and smacked his lips. He then asked, 'Any more?' Terry refilled the glass and poured the remainder into Alicia's. 'Cheers,' said George. 'Thank you,' said Alicia sweetly. Just as they were about to leave, George handed us his bottle (a small one!) 'Thank you,' said Terry, with an amused look on his face.

'What the hell are you playing at,' I asked, after they had gone. 'Why did you give them the whole bottle?' Terry just shrugged his shoulders.

We had spent a couple of hours playing snakes and ladders with George's sister when the door was violently flung open and George ran in. I saw that his face was pale, but without speaking he flung his jacket on to the floor and galloped out again.

I looked at Terry – who seemed to have difficulty in keeping a straight face – and asked, 'What the devil is up with him?'

'Search me,' he answered.

George returned about fifteen minutes later, holding his belly and looking even paler than before, and, still without speaking, he went into his bedroom. When he came back out I saw that he had changed his trousers. 'What's the matter?' I asked. He emitted a groan, and, looking at me with pain-filled eyes, he replied, 'I've got the bloody skitters!'

I was about to commiserate with him when, with a howl of pain, he jumped to his feet and fled through the front door once more, and when he returned about half an hour later he looked completely exhausted.

Still clutching his belly, he sat on the settee and then he wailed, 'That's not the worst of it.'

'What do you mean?' I asked.

With a sob he replied, 'It's Alicia, I think she has filled her knickers.'

I roared with laughter at the thought of haughty Alicia losing control of her bowels.

'How can you be sure of that?' I asked.

With a choked voice he replied, 'Well, when we left the cinema, she suddenly clasped her stomach and said, "Oh my God," and then hurried to the ladies' toilets. While I waited for her to return I got a sudden severe pain in my guts, and before I could do anything about it I shit myself. I had to run all the way home!'

It was altogether too much for Terry and I – we rolled on the floor laughing! We saw the reproach in George's eyes, so Terry, most solicitously, said, 'What a shame. It must have been something you both ate.'

George looked the picture of abject misery when we left him, but once outside Terry began to cackle.

'What the hell have you been up to?' I asked.

'Jallop!' he replied.

Then the penny dropped. 'You don't mean—?'

He nodded. 'Aye, there was enough in that bottle to give a horse the runs!'

Well, Alicia was missing for days – no doubt nursing a sore bottom – and when she finally reappeared she cut George dead.

That dirty trick must have been one of the best-kept secrets of all time – the victims were never to learn the cause of their embarrassment.

My sincere apologies to both of you, if you're reading this.

Chapter Forty-One

'Have you given any thought to your future?' asked Mother.

'Some,' I replied.

'Your compensation stops next week.'

'I know that.'

'Well, what are you going to do?'

'What would you like me to do, go down another pit?'

'Don't be nasty!'

'I'm not being nasty, but I ceased to think about the future when I was persuaded to take a job at Elswick.'

Actually, I had given a great deal of thought to it, but during those idle months I had also pondered deeply about the previous two years. I was in no doubt that they had been completely wasted because I had absolutely nothing to show for them – except that I had been scarred by three terrifying experiences whilst working underground!

There I was, in my seventeenth year, unskilled and with a pretty hopeless future to look forward to. Despite my acceptance of the fact that I was destined to become a manual worker (honest though it was) I still felt a fierce resentment at having been denied the opportunity to carve out a career of my choosing.

My hand had healed but I didn't regain full use of it until I had endured some extremely painful physiotherapy and electric treatment, but the doctors had assured me that it would not cause me any great inconvenience,

despite the flattened knuckles. Yet for a long time afterwards I had frightful nightmares in which I relived those
few minutes of agony and terror at the shaft-bottom of
Elswick Colliery.

Once again Granddad proposed to pull a few strings
and get me a job in an electrical factory. He put it very
nicely too! 'There will be plenty of brainwork but that
shouldn't bother you too much.'

I didn't hesitate. 'Sorry Granddad, but I was denied the
opportunity of using my brain two years ago, so I don't
want to use it now.' Naturally he took umbridge and
'washed his bloody hands of me!'

Of course I was wrong in adopting such a churlish
attitude, and it hadn't gone down too well with Mother,
who didn't hesitate to voice her anger.

What did the future hold for me? It was by pure
chance that some of my problems were solved – at least
for the foreseeable future.

I had been to the colliery to collect my final compensation payment when, on the way back, I passed a painter
scraping away at a garden gate. After I had gone a few
yards I realised I had seen him before, then the penny
dropped – of course, he had been a friend of Dad and I
had last seen him in the cemetery.

I doubled back. 'Hello, Mr Maule,' I said. Now, that
man possessed a most remarkable memory, because, after
gazing at me for just a few seconds, he replied, 'Are you
young Herbert?' I was!

Well, the outcome of that encounter was Mr Maule
visiting Mother and my beginning an apprenticeship as a
painter and decorator.

★ ★ ★

The remainder of 1925 was marked by a misfortune that
had overtaken Granddad – one that caused a rare old
panic.

The first inclination we at home had of his trouble came when we had a visitor from the health department.

'Your name Herbert?' the bloke asked Mother.

'Yes.'

'Your father's named Henderson?'

'Yes.'

'When was he here last?'

'A week ago, but who are you and why the questions about my father?'

'He's in hospital.'

'What?'

'An isolation hospital.'

'My God, what's wrong with him?' bawled Ma.

'He has smallpox.'

'Eh?'

'He is suffering from smallpox!'

'Oh Jesus,' moaned Ma.

'You and your family have to be vaccinated.'

'Oh no!'

'Oh yes,' retorted our visitor. 'A doctor will be here shortly so remain indoors until he has examined you.'

Unpleasant news always travelled at lightening speed in The Avenue, and it wasn't long before the locals were spitting out their unique brand of sympathy.

'Now they have brought the fuckin' plague!'

'Fancy bringing their spots among us decent people!'

You have to believe me when I tell you that those comments comprised only a tiny part of the repertoire of our dear neighbours.

The incubation period did cause us some anxiety, but fortunately none of us had contracted the disease.

However, let me dwell for a while on something a little more pleasant – bowlers. No, not the kind who trundle a black ball along a stretch of grass and then gallop after it, hoping to persuade the damn thing to make contact with a small white one. I am referring to the kind one wears on one's head. You know, bowler hats!

Before I go any further I would like to refer to a certain gentleman popularly called 'the ragman'. He used to pay regular visits to the area with a barrow piled high with used clothing. He was always a welcome visitor because most of the community could only afford to buy second-hand articles. (It didn't matter if the bloomers and long-john's had previously draped the dirty bums of God only knows who – they could be washed, couldn't they?)

And this is where my unpredictable friend Terry crops up again; he called on me one Saturday evening carrying a large paper bag.

'What have you got in there?' I asked.

'Two hats,' he replied.

'Two hats?'

'Aye, booler hats.' (No, it is not a mistake, he said booler!)

'Where did you get them?'

'Off the ragman—'

'What are you going to do with them?'

'—and there is one for you.'

'What am I going to do with a bowler, pee in it?'

'I'm going to wear one—'

'You are what?'

'—and I want you to wear the other one.'

Of course I had to laugh at the absurdity of the idea. 'Me wear a bowler?' I gasped, 'You must be mad!'

He didn't answer but took one of them from the bag and solemnly stuck it onto his head; he then postured in front of the mirror, carefully viewing the 'booler' from various angles. 'How do I look?' he asked. I couldn't answer for laughing!

He handed me the other one. 'Here, try this on for size.' I had to enter into the spirit of the occasion so I stuck the bowler on my head – I looked dafter than he did! 'It suits you,' he said, with an approving nod.

At that moment a warning bell sounded in my head. 'Just what are you up to?' I asked him.

'I am going tashing on Sunday.'

'What are you talking about?'

'And I want you to come with me.'

'You want me to do what?'

'And wear that booler.'

I was beginning to have my doubts about my pal's sanity. 'Are you feeling alright?' I asked him.

'Listen,' he replied, 'Let's have a bit of fun. If we take a walk up the North Road tomorrow night we are sure to touch for a bit of crumpet, that is why I paid a tanner for the bleeding boolers!'

'You can bugger off,' I shouted.

'Howway man, it's only a lark.'

'Listen,' I said, 'You look a freak, I look a freak, so who the hell will look at a couple of freaks?'

However, despite my protests and misgivings, I found myself sauntering up the North Road feeling – and no doubt looking – a proper Charlie!

One thing we had not dared to do was wear the flaming boolers in The Avenue, such an act of folly would certainly have evoked a storm of ridicule. We therefore carried the things in the paper bag until we reached Percy Street, where, after a good look round, we furtively stuck them on our heads. Then we sallied forth, looking for likely talent – and by golly there was plenty of it!

'Hello gorgeous,' cooed Terry when a couple of lasses approached us. They stopped and looked at us, then bolted!

We made further effort a few minutes later, but one of the girls just sniffed and the other said succinctly, 'Get lost!'

I was becoming disenchanted but Terry was a glutton for punishment. 'Hello beautiful,' he said heartily to another couple of girls. Well, at least they didn't sniff and run away! The two girls looked at us (and judging by the look of awe on their faces, I was sure we had scored!)

Then, after some moments of embarrassing silence, one of them said to me, 'Who are you supposed to be?' There was no answer to that! The other one, who had been scrutinising Terry very closely, said to him. 'You have forgotten your little moustache, Charlie!'

I heard my slighted friend growling so I grabbed him and hustled him towards the plantation, into which I flung the blasted bowlers.

I snarled at him, 'Good for a laugh, you said!'

'Charlie Chaplin eh, fuckin' Charlie Chaplin she called me,' he hooted.

'Come on, let's hop it,' I said.

'It was all your fault anyway,' he yelled.

'What the hell do you mean?'

'You looked like Marley's ghost in that fuckin' booler, that's what!'

What a pal!

Chapter Forty-Two

Mr Maule was truly an amazing man. He was not only a master painter but also an accomplished violinist, and even more astonishing was his knowledge of Greek mythology, which he said had fascinated him from childhood. But most of all he was an excellent tutor and I could not have been in better hands.

In every way it was an education working for him. Having elicited that I was very fond of music, he would extol the merits of famous composers, and if he thought a change was needed he would switch to his favourite subject – Greeks and their myths!

The fact that he was a very brainy man prompted me to ask him why he hadn't put his talents to better use. His reply astonished me.

'I had to leave school when I was only twelve years old,' he began. 'There were ten of us in my family and father was a cripple. My first job was as an errand boy, for which I received the princely sum of 2/6 per week. I had always wanted to go to a good school but I had the family to think about, so it was out of the question. I used to save every ha'penny I could and when I was fourteen I paid for my first violin lesson. When I was sixteen, my tutor sent me to a music school for testing, with a view to becoming a pupil, and I was lucky enough to be accepted. Unfortunately, just before I was due to start the first term, my parents both died within weeks of each other, leaving eight kids of whom I was the eldest. So I put my music behind me and started work as an apprentice painter. My knowledge of mythology was attained simply by reading books on the subject. My life has been a happy one and I have no regrets. Who knows, had I qualified as a first class musician I might have been bloody miserable!'

I often thought about that remarkable man's philosophy, how he had accepted without rancour the knowledge that his musical career was to be denied him, and how cheerfully he had shouldered the burden of caring for his family. There was a lesson in that for me.

I was making excellent progress as an apprentice under him when the unbelievable happened – he collapsed and died of a heart attack. So, when the business closed, I was back to square one.

The following week Terry suggested I go and see his boss, who was looking for some lads, and having nothing to lose, I agreed.

I made my way to Cowgate the following morning – that's where the site was situated – and I found it to be a huge estate, which stretched for miles. I walked round and round the damn place looking for Terry, but there was no sign of him.

After about an hour, I decided to call it a day and began to retrace my steps to the main road, but just as I was about to leave the estate I spotted a man in white overalls standing outside a shed, so I went up to him and asked whether he was needing any hands. 'Yes,' he replied, 'Have you any experience at mixing?' 'Plenty,' I said. (Mr Maule had showed me how to mix paints and I was quite good at it.) 'Right,' said the man, 'Start in the morning.'

Terry was puzzled. 'What's the name of the firm,' he asked me.

'I've no idea, why?'

'I thought we were the only painters on the site,' he replied.

'Well, you can't be, because I'm starting in the morning.'

Of course I would have to sleep in, and I arrived on the job at least half an hour late, where I found the shed locked. (I should mention that it was one of numerous sheds situated some considerable distance from where the building was taking place.)

To my relief I saw my new boss walking towards me, and after brushing aside my apology for being late, he unlocked the door of the shed.

'Right,' said the man, 'Grab a shovel.'

'Shovel?'

'Aye, shovel.'

'What do I want with a shovel?'

'You can't work without one, can you?'

'I can't paint with one either!'

'Eh?'

'It will be difficult dipping a shovel into a paint-pot!'

'Blimey, are you a painter?' asked the man.

'Yes, I am.'

'Fuckin' hell, I want somebody to work on a concrete mixer!'

I was lost for words. I realised of course that his white overalls had deceived me into thinking he was a painter.

We both saw the funny side of a ridiculous situation, but having enjoyed a good laugh I asked him, 'What is the wage for the job?'

'Twenty-five bob, and overtime if you want it.'

Now that made me think, because it would be almost twice what I would get as an apprentice painter – and I acted impulsively. 'I'll take it,' I said.

Ten minutes later I was shovelling sand and cement into a bloody big mixer, and ten hours later I was ruefully licking my blistered hands!

For about two months I fed the gaping maw of that hungry mixer, until I learned that the boss was notorious for employing youths instead of adults, so I gave it the old heave-ho and departed for pastures new.

Mother threw a fit when I told her. 'Just what are you going to do now?' she yelled.

To tell the truth, I didn't know what I was going to do; I had set my sights on something a little more reward-ing than being a miner, a painter or a builder's labourer. All honest occupations maybe (after all, Dad had been a miner) but where was the sense of achievement?

But the difficulties I would have to face in order to obtain decent employment were driven home after the mixer lark, as the following story illustrates.

Terry and I were on our way to the Empire one Friday night and, as we passed Jackson the Tailor, I noticed a sign hanging in the window: 'Youth wanted for training as salesman.'

'I think I will have a go at that,' I said to my pal.

'You are joking.'

'I am not.'

'Only puffs work in those places.'

'Then I will be a puff!'

So I brushed my suit, my shoes and my teeth and set off with hope in my heart the following morning for Jackson's. (Mother had sniggered when I told her of my intention.)

'I have called about the vacancy, Sir,' I said politely.

'How old are you?' asked the skinny-faced floor manager.

'Sixteen and a half, nearly seventeen.'

'Hmm.'

(At this point I would like to say that the floor man-ager had an Adam's apple as big as a duck egg – I was fascinated by it bobbing up and down.)

'Have you had any experience in this trade?'

'No, Sir.'

'What school did you attend?'

'Cambridge Street.'

'Never heard of it.' (Pause.) 'Is it a grammar school?'

'No, Sir.'

I had been unable to take my eyes away from that bouncing lump on his throat and I must have half smiled because he suddenly barked, 'What are you laughing at?'

'I am not laughing, Sir.'

'Have you had any kind of higher education?'

'No, Sir.'

'Then you are no good to me,' he snapped.

By then the fluctuations of that gigantic Adam's apple had proved too much for me – I gave a hearty belly laugh! But when the irate man made a grab for me I beat a hasty retreat.

Oh yes, the handicap of having an inferior education was going to prove difficult to overcome. For the moment it was back to painting.

It was shortly after the fiasco at Jackson's that an incident concerning Terry occurred – one that distressed me not a little.

Among the many records we then possessed was one that played a mournful song called 'When you played the organ and I sang the Rosary'. One evening when I was alone in the house I put it on by mistake, and just before it began to play there was a knock on the door and Terry walked in. I turned to him to say something but then a funereal voice came through the horn of the gramophone, churning out the awful dirge. To my consternation, I saw him cover his face with his hands and begin to sob uncontrollably.

To see my tough friend crying like that was not only unusual but quite upsetting, so I quickly stopped the gramophone and went to him. 'Hey lad, what's up?' I asked. I had to wait before he was able to answer. 'My mother died an hour ago.'

Well, I fully understood his grief because she had always tried to protect him from his brothers and their beatings, but witnessing his tears made me realise just how much that lad had been misunderstood, for beneath that tough façade was a tender nature.

It brought to mind his answer when I had once asked him why he used so much bad language. 'I used to be treated as though I was a mangy dog; I never knew what a kind word was until your family moved here. Remember the time your father bathed the cuts on my back? Well, that was the time my family wanted to put me away – I wasn't wanted. I had become a loner and no-one has offered me friendship except you and your family. I try hard not to swear too much – I have to confess in church every morning – but the only way I can express my feelings sometimes is by telling people to fuck off!'

Those were the bitter thoughts of a young man soured by brutality; a youth who needed only to be shown a little affection and understanding.

After another week of idleness I began to regret my packing-in of the mixer job – well, just a little!

'I told you, didn't I, clever bugger,' said Mother. (Yes she was upset, but not half as much as she was going to be a few days later.)

I had taken a casual stroll to the juvenile bureau, hoping there would be a job of some kind going (Terry's boss didn't need any more lads) and did I get a surprise.

'You're an apprentice painter?' asked the clerk.

'Yes.'

'A local contractor needs a couple of lads, do you want to go?'

'Thank you, yes.'

'It's only for four weeks.'

'I understand.'

'You will have to work in Carstairs.'

'Where's that?'

'Scotland.'

'Eh?'

'Scotland. Do you still wish to go?'

'Certainly!'

Mother really blew her gasket when I told her. She

could have stopped me, of course, because I was a minor, but she didn't.

There were eight men and two lads in the party when we left the Central on the Monday morning en-route to Carlisle, where we met the contractor who accompanied us for the remainder of the journey to Carstairs.

I learned that the job was government-sponsored for the benefit of ex-servicemen. Thousands of acres of land adjacent to Carstairs had been divided into smallholdings and a new house had been built on each – which we were to paint.

Lodgings had been arranged for us (I was closeted with a kindly couple) and the cost was met from a government fund. I never knew how much the men were paid, but us lads were given a pound pocket money, which was a good sum in those days. I had made no arrangements with Mother regarding money, so I decided to save as much as I could and take it back with me.

So, for four glorious weeks I worked in the heart of the beautiful Scottish countryside, where there were no lice or bedbugs and where the people, albeit God-fearing, were warm and friendly. Even the rain descended in clear sparkling drops, quite unlike the dirty water that fell on The Avenue and besmirched everything it touched.

Those four weeks passed all too quickly, and I had no sooner set foot back in the stinking Avenue when I sensed trouble – and how right I was. I hadn't informed Ma when I would return, so she hardly expected me to walk in and find her in the middle of a crying bout.

'I'm glad you're home,' she sniffed.

'What's up?'

'It's your Aunt Bella.'

'What about her?'

'She has hopped it!'

'Hopped it?'

'Yes, with another man!'

'Serve him right.'

'It's no laughing matter,' she yelled.

'It is to me, she once called me a snotty young bugger, remember?'

However, it *was* an extremely serious affair because Bella's husband had promptly followed her example, which meant there were nine bewildered children left alone. Eventually, six of them – to their parents' eternal shame – ended their childhood in Dr Banardo's home.

The scandalmongers in The Avenue had a ready-made target for their verbal attacks – my Mother.

I immediately called on Fred and found him in an angry mood. He told me that not only had Mother been getting hell, but he too had been involved in a great deal of unpleasantness – verging almost on violence at times.

I could well imagine the nastiness of the gossip, but I realised that no useful purpose would be served by getting involved in arguments that would eventually lead to violence, and there was no way I wanted him to tangle with The Avenue louts. So, hard though it would prove to be, I persuaded him to ignore the comments.

In the meantime, though, my first priority was to find a job, and once again Terry offered to assist, and the following week I started work alongside him at Cowgate. There was the prospect of a long run of work, and besides, Christmas wasn't too far away and I didn't want to be skint during the festive season.

Working with him gave me a greater insight into the workings of his mind. Unlike me (a dreamer) he lived only for the moment, and his main object in life was to enjoy every one of them. He had no interest in traveling or faraway places, canny Newcastle was good enough for him!

The very end of 1925 was memorable only because of a scene between Ma and I. It started after I had been talking at great length with Fred and he had asked, 'Any chance of you going away again?' I had replied, 'I don't think so, why?'

It was obvious that something was bothering him and there was a long pause before he answered, 'Well, I have told you before that Mother may marry again and you are not likely to accept a stepfather, are you?'

I have to admit that I wasn't unduly worried whether she married or not; after all, I was almost eighteen years old and my determination to leave The Avenue at the first opportunity was stronger than ever. But I decided (unwisely) to sound her out on the subject – and she almost hit the bloody ceiling!

'Have you, like Fred, been listening to gossip?'

'No.'

'Then mind your own flaming business.'

'You know what the gossips have already done to you,' I said.

'Bugger them, I will please myself what I do.' And that was that.

But I had to tell her that if she remarried I would wish her well, but I would leave home immediately.

I wasn't to know that a similar personal discussion would take place between us not long afterwards – but the positions would be reversed!

Chapter Forty-Three

It was near the end of 1925 when young Jim decided to climb a high tree in Elswick Park. He had scaled it with ease but then he thought he would do a Tarzan act – and promptly fell to the ground.

He was brought home badly shaken but otherwise unscathed, by a girl of about my age whose name, I learned, was Angela.

Now, if that silly young sod had not fallen from that tree, and if I had not been gallant enough to escort the girl home, then there would have been no story.

She was quite attractive and I suppose I was rather flattered when she agreed to go for a walk with me. But after a few weeks it became obvious that we had very little in common.

Angela had a mania for walking and dancing, and I hated the latter and couldn't be bothered to do much of the former, but she expected me to tote her all over the place every bloomin' night.

I eventually made it clear that I was much too tired at night to do much walking, although I was prepared to go for a short walk maybe at weekends.

Angela, however, was nothing if not persistent. No matter what time of the evening, when I would leave the house, there she was. 'I was just passing!'

One evening I got browned off and asked Terry to

have a look and see if she was knocking about, and if she was, to tell her I was sick, and if that didn't work to say that I had emigrated. He was having none of that! 'You can bugger off, go and tell her yourself.'

About a week after that refusal, he asked me something that made me jump. 'Sam,' he asked with a smirk, 'Have you plinked Angela's plonk?'

'What the hell do you mean?' I asked, outraged.

'Have you plinked her plonk?' he repeated.

'No I have not you scruffy sod!'

'Well, every bugger in The Avenue thinks you have her in the family way, and that's why she's running after you.'

'You're joking?'

'No, I'm not. In fact, I could have told you weeks ago about the gossip.'

I was horrified, but I should have expected it because, for those responsible for most of the filthy gossip, there was no such thing as a clean friendship between the sexes. Added to that was the fact that my name was Herbert, which, along with the scandal concerning Bella, gave them a little extra to talk about.

I realised that I would have to scotch the rumours by eliminating the cause of it – I would have to finish with Angela immediately.

And it was then that Mother got her own back.

'What's this I hear about that girl of yours?' she snapped.

'What have you heard?' I asked, rather loudly.

'That she's pregnant.'

'It's a flaming lie,' I retorted.

'Is it?'

'Yes!'

'Well, as you said to me, you know what the gossips are like.'

Touché!

Even Fred believed I had put one in the oven.

'Listen, Fred,' I yelled, 'Nothing like that has happened.'

'Are you serious about her?'

'No! In fact, I'm going to send her packing.'

'Then hurry up and do it and put a stop to all the bloody gossip!'

I didn't feel too happy the following evening when my grinning pal Terry poked his head around our kitchen door and said, 'Get your skates on Sam, here she comes!'

This is it, I thought, as I went out to meet Angela. I had rehearsed my breaking-off speech and all I had to do was to deliver it.

I watched as she walked towards me, smiling, and I wondered what the hell she was so happy about.

Her first words sounded like 'On the way' and I almost fell down the steps with shock!

'What did you say?' I whispered.

'I'm going away,' she repeated.

'Oh! Where to?' I asked, very, very relieved.

'Manchester. I'm going for training as a dancer.'

'When do you go?' I asked, trying to hide my elation.

'Tomorrow.'

My delight at her leaving was dampened a little when she asked, 'Will you write to me?' It flashed though my mind that if I were to say no there was the possibility of her changing her mind, so, with ardent sincerity, I answered, 'Of course I will.' (Like hell I would!)

She had been gone about three weeks when a letter arrived from her. I was informed of its arrival by young Jim. 'There is a letter for you, it must be from that tart of yours,' for which observation he received a kick up the arse.

I slowly read it, and in her own words she was having a bloody good time, so in view of that I decided to let her get on with it and ignore the letter.

To my dismay, another letter arrived the following week, and once again she wrote about the marvellous time she was having. My conscience didn't bother me when I ignored that one too.

Yet I wondered why I had turned against the girl with such finality. I could have blamed the vicious gossip, or even the manner in which she chased after me, but that wouldn't have been true because I had become aware of my aversion for her before that. But there was certainly something about her that didn't click with me, and when I compared her to my friend Irene, she just didn't measure up.

I had to do the decent thing by writing to her and telling her not to write again, but before I could do so, another one arrived.

It was lying on the table when I came home from work, and Mother must have been getting herself worked up because I had ignored the previous ones. 'If I was that girl,' she said, jabbing the letter with a fork, 'I would spit in your bloody eye the next time I saw you!' She didn't give me time to make any comment. 'That is the third letter the poor girl has written to you. What are you going to do about it?' Rather feebly I answered, 'I'm writing to her this week.' She just sniffed.

I opened the envelope and began to read the contents, then I quickly re-read it. 'My dearest pig-face,' it started, but after reading just a few lines I hurriedly folded it up and put it in my pocket.

'Something wrong?' asked Mother, who had been watching me closely.

'No, it's just a short letter,' I lied.

I waited until I was in the seclusion of my box-room before reading it right through, and when I reached the end I just sat there dumbfounded, because the letter was one long sentence of vituperation, with almost every other word an obscenity!

Even allowing for the fact that I had deserved a strong letter from Angela, I found it hard to believe that such filth could have emanated from the pen of a girl I once thought to be nice! (What had Mother said? 'The poor girl'!)

Terry whistled when I showed the letter to him. 'You should have plinked her plonk,' he said. 'You have a one-track mind,' I snapped back.

I burned the letter with the consoling thought that there would be no more letters from her, but swipe me if she didn't write again the following week expressing her regrets and would I meet her at the Palace the following Monday, where she was dancing in the chorus. (Not on your Nellie.)

On the Sunday morning I was enjoying a lie-in when young Jim poked his head round the door and yelled, 'Hey our Sammy, you're wanted at the door.'

'Who is it,' I asked, sleepily.

'It's that tart of yours.'

'What did you say?' I yelped in disbelief.

'It's your tart,' he gleefully shouted.

I scrambled out of bed, pulled my pants on, and gave a furtive peep through the curtains. What I saw made my hair stand on end.

It was Angela all right, but oh my God! She was wearing a large hat, she had a fur stole round her neck, and she was balancing herself on a pair of heels at least six inches high! As if she didn't look ridiculous enough, she was absolutely plastered with make-up, and the over-generous application of lipstick gave her mouth the appearance of an exaggerated pout!

I simply had to get her away from the front door before the neighbours got their eyes on her, so I grabbed my jacket and went out, followed by words of comfort from Ma, who had been watching with some amusement. 'Serves you right!' she chortled.

I grabbed Angela and almost ran out of The Avenue and when we reached Rye Hill I stopped and had a good look at her. I didn't tell her she looked ridiculous because I remembered the letter she had sent me, but I couldn't help wondering what the hell had come over her.

But I was really staggered when she began to tell me about her life on the stage because her language was foul. I was no paragon of virtue, but to have to listen to such profanity from a girl I had once liked was particularly nauseating. It was time to say goodbye.

She listened in silence when I told her what was on my mind, but when I finished she twisted her mouth and sneered, 'Well, go on then, piss off pig-face!'

Then she delivered a devastating parting shot as I turned away from her, 'You don't know what the fuckin' thing is for, do you?'

You know something? She hurt my feelings!

Anyhow, some geezer who obviously knew what it was for really plinked her plonk – she rolled home some months later with a baby.

Chapter Forty-Four

The year 1925 was a good one in many ways. Both Terry and I had been working regularly and I was managing to save a few bob each week, but that elusive day when I could leave The Avenue for good seemed as far away as ever.

If any event could be termed surprising it was the fact that Fred had joined the Territorials!

'What on earth made you join that mob?' I asked him.

'Well,' he replied, 'There is an annual two-week camp at Ripon and many weekends are spent under canvas, and God knows I could do with the fresh air.'

I looked at him because he had never indulged in bitterness regarding his life, and I sensed that for once he was telling me that he was tired of the kind of life he had to endure.

He would not have thanked me for any sympathy, so I asked him, 'Fred, do you ever get sick of this bloody hole?'

'Yes,' he replied, 'But what the hell can I do about it?'

'I know how you feel,' I said, 'Because we both detested the place the day we entered it, but after nearly eleven years I am fed up with it all and I am not going to waste any more time than I can help living in it. There are times when I could scream in sheer frustration as I lie in that pokey, dark box-room. I have no intention of allowing myself to drift into the zombie-like state of hopelessness which has been the inevitable end for most young men in this area.'

Fred smiled at my vehement outburst, and then, a little wistfully, he said, 'If I was a healthy young bugger like you I would be out of this place in a flash.'

A couple of days later I was standing with Terry at the bottom of Rye Hill when a youth in naval uniform approached. I recognised him as a former Hazelrigg mate.

'When did you join the Navy?' I asked him.

'Not the Navy, the naval reserve.'

He told me quite a lot about it and as he left he said, 'Why not join?'

Well, that was something worth thinking about and a few weeks later I casually asked Terry, 'What about joining the naval reserve?' He grimaced and replied, 'Listen chum, if you think I'm going to fanny about in a fuckin' sailor's uniform then you have another thing coming!'

I continued to give it serious thought and eventually I went to the training ship and had another talk with my ex-miner friend. I made my mind up that evening and I joined the RNVR the following week. (I can still see the amazed look on Mother's face when I walked in with a kitbag full of uniforms!)

'You're determined to get away, aren't you?' she yelled. I tried to explain the reason for joining but she wouldn't listen, even though I told her my motives were the same as Fred's, it made no bloody difference. 'You only think about yourself, to hell with us!'

Sadly, she thought that I was a selfish young sod, when nothing could have been further from the truth. My desire to leave The Avenue didn't mean I had no affection for my family, nor that I was trying to shirk my responsibilities. But I did have my own life to carve out, and I was determined to do it.

Terry asked me the same question I had asked Fred. 'What made you join?'

'Listen,' I replied, 'The lad I was speaking to that night had just returned from a training period with the fleet, and during those fourteen weeks he had been to the West Indies, North Africa, Spain and the Bahamas. So you see, he saw a bit of the world *and* got paid for it!'

The headquarters of the reserves was an old wooden man-o-war moored alongside a jetty adjoining Vickers' factory. Its official name was HMS *Calliope* and it had a complement of about two hundred men, who came from all walks of life.

Incidentally, I had lied about my age because I was not then eighteen years old, and I had taken a chance on stalling them for a couple of months before producing my birth certificate.

It was inevitable that my joining the reserve would soon become common knowledge, and it followed that I would be a target, not only for good-natured banter, but also for sneering comments, when I made my first appearance in uniform. Sure enough, they let me have it!

'Big head!'

'Seasick Horbat!' (How my name was pronounced!)

'Weekend sailor!'

'Little boy blue!'

Terry was standing at his door and I paused to have a chat with him, and after he had given me the 'once over' he winked and said, 'You look smart kidder!' Praise indeed!

Fred's reaction was similar, but he also said, 'This will be your first step to getting away from here, won't it?' I nodded. 'Then why don't you join the regular navy when you're eighteen?' But he well knew that the uncertainty of home was the stumbling block. Young Jim and Dora were only eight and ten years old, and I couldn't leave them to the mercy of the parish.

My first training period on board the ship was in the nature of a Cook's tour; there were six of us, all rookies, and we learned to distinguish the sharp end of the ship from the blunt end. We were taught the rudiments of marching, and after about an hour we fell-out to have a smoke.

I was standing with my back to the gangway, wondering what I had let myself in for, when a voice broke through my thoughts. 'How do I join this mob?'

Startled, I swung round to face the owner of the voice. 'What the hell are you doing here?' I gasped. 'I've come to join,' said a sheepish-looking Terry. I shook my head in disbelief, but I guided him to the ship's office.

He was waiting for me on the jetty. 'How did you get on?' I asked eagerly. 'Nothing to it, and I've passed the doctor.'

So there we were, two pals whose lives were about to undergo a radical change – for the better.

Yet only a few days later we were involved in an incident which not only threatened to terminate our naval careers before they had even begun, but brought home to us how far-reaching the stigma of residing in the infamous Avenue really was.

It is only in recent years that most forms of gambling have become legalised. In my young days there were no such places as betting shops, and that was why almost every back lane was used as a stand-by street bookies. To counteract the unwelcome attention of crafty plain-clothed police officers, the bookies employed lookouts, or touts, who were posted at various street corners. Obviously they were a priority target for the coppers, particularly a certain detective by the name of Meddler.

The incident I refer to took place as Terry and I were walking up Rye Hill one Saturday afternoon. We crossed Sycamore Street and noticed a queue standing outside a narrow entrance, which meant that there was a bookie inside – probably paying some winning punters.

Suddenly we heard a yell and saw the queue scatter, some of which came charging towards us. We jumped out of the path of the stampede and as we did so we saw Meddler come charging towards us. He damn near broke

Terry's neck with a wicked half nelson and I was suddenly grabbed by the scruff. 'You're both nicked,' snarled Meddler. 'What the bleeding hell for?' gurgled Terry. 'You are both charged with touting,' was the answer. Despite our protests, we were marched along Scotswood Road to the local nick, where we were flung into a cell. We were hauled out half an hour later by a fifteen stone, poe-faced police sergeant.

Oddly enough, Terry had said very little during the humiliating episode, but I could see by the expression on his face that he had almost reached boiling point and I began to worry, because I knew that any violent reaction by him could only have serious repercussions.

'Names?' barked the beefy sergeant.

'Herbert.'

'Muckian.'

'Address?'

'The Avenue.'

The sergeant flung down his pen. 'I might have known because you fuckin' lot from that place are all the fuckin' same.' After a pause he nodded to a subordinate, 'Put these two bastards back inside.'

'You can't do that,' I said heatedly, 'We're not touts and never have been!'

'I can't eh?' snarled the then purple-faced sergeant, jumping to his feet (only then did I realise just how massive he was!). He learned over the desk, grabbed me by the neck, and lifted me off the floor. Then he began to shake me as though I was a baby's rattle! At last, when my teeth were ready to drop out, he released me.

There was a surprise development though as we were being ushered back to the cells, when there arrived in the station the luckless bookie in the grip of two coppers. But that damned sergeant was reluctant to accept the bookie's assertion that he had never seen us before, and a further hour was to elapse before we were finally released.

We left the police station with some 'friendly' advice ringing in our ears. 'We shall be watching you two tykes, and if ever you are brought in here again, you will be for it!'

Such an incident illustrates the difficulties faced by decent people who longed only to better themselves but were denied the opportunity of doing so because they lived in the wrong place.

'You live where? The Avenue? Sorry chum!'

Chapter Forty-Five

It wasn't easy persuading Terry to walk down The
Avenue in uniform for the first time – he knew what to
expect. But the loud-mouthed clever-dick who shouted,
'Up your hawse-pipe, Muckian,' didn't. After Terry had
finished with him his 'hawse-pipe' was sore for a long
time afterwards! And there were no more catcalls.

As was to be expected, it took a little time for us to
understand what naval life was all about, but when we settled down and became fully acquainted with the rest of
the men, life became easier. Although we had to attend
officially only twice a week, the ship was open every night
to the crew. There was a fully licensed bar, a gymnasium,
and if anyone felt like some strenuous exercise, the small
boats were lowered and rowed upstream and back.

The instructors were all regular Chief Petty Officers,
and, depending on your ability, you were taught Gunnery,
Signalling or Torpedoes. But first we had to be taught
how to march and that was carried out on the jetty.

'Pick 'em up,' bawled the instructor.

'Bollax!' said a voice. (Guess who?)

Then there was the rifle drill; a series of intricate
manoeuvres that left Terry stone cold. 'Why do I have
to chuck this bloody thing all over the place?' he asked
a startled officer, who, I am sure, couldn't think of an
appropriate answer.

His pet hate, though, was learning to make knots and splicing. I well remember one evening when we were being taught to tie an intricate knot called a sheepshank. After a few demonstrations, we were each given a length of rope with which to practise.

Well, not everybody got it right the first time, or the second, in fact it was beyond some of the class – and that included Terry. He got himself into an awful tangle, and his patience was almost at an end when the instructor asked him to show the result. My friend held up the sorry-looking tangled mass of cord. 'What the hell's that?' asked the befuddled officer.

'Well,' answered a straight-faced Terry, 'If it's not a sheepshank, it could be a brush-shank or a ham-shank, or any fuckin' shank you like!' Even the instructor had to join in the uproarious laughter that followed. Indeed, as time went on, Terry was to become a popular member of the ship's company because of his ready wit and down-to-earth expressions.

Every man had to be proficient in seamanship, and that included, among other things, the art of 'boxing the compass' and learning the rules of the sea. It was also a 'must' that each man learned by heart the meaning of the various sailing lights that ships display when in the open sea.

In order that recruits should understand and remember the many and complicated rules, a unique method of instruction was used. This took the form of 'doggerels' and every man was given a series of them to learn by heart.

One of those odd poems went something like this:

GREEN TO GREEN OR RED TO RED
PERFECT SAFETY; GO AHEAD

Nothing difficult about that you may say. No? Read on.

There were about thirty recruits in the class, each of whom had been diligently digesting those doggerels –

and testing time had come. Terry jumped like a startled buck when the examining officer pointed a finger at him. 'You, read and explain doggerel number one.' (That is the one I have given as an example above.)

An alarmed Terry rose to his feet, looked around him, scratched his head, looked at the ceiling for inspiration, then self-consciously began, 'Er, Green to Green or Red to Red,' (a long pause). 'Go on man!' bawled the impatient officer. Terry smiled and continued, 'Er, Violets are blue, roses are red, sod you mate, I'm off to bed!' The whole class erupted into laughter. Even the examiner laughed out loud. You know, with such an innate sense of sponta-neous wit, how could Terry be anything but popular?

As 1926 drew to a close we began to spend almost all our spare time on board, with Terry doing his stuff in the boxing ring and I devoting myself to rifle shooting. My pal was never happy unless he was knocking the stuffing out of some poor bugger in the ring, and he jumped at the chance to take part in a sporting contest – an annual event between the *Calliope* and her sister ship *Satellite*, which was stationed at North Shields. Among the many events was boxing, and Terry had been selected to repre-sent us in one of the bouts.

Such contests were mostly at catch-weights, and Terry's reaction when he saw his opponent was typical – 'Blimey, he's a six-foot fuckin' hairpin!' But things were not as they seemed.

Come the first round and Terry, bobbing and weav-ing, went confidently into battle. He led with his left and clipped his opponent neatly in the goolies! The outraged man, who was at least two feet taller than Terry, yelped and backed away. I noticed that the hairpin had arms about six feet long, and as Terry moved forward again he was confronted by a windmill! 'It's like fighting a friggin' octopus!' Terry snorted.

Then came the second round and Terry jumped up from his stool, hoping to catch the big bloke before those long arms started twirling, but something went wrong. From out of the blue there came a long tentacle with a glove on the end of it, which smacked him square in the mush!

With his jaw hanging open, Terry sat on his bum wondering what the hell had hit him. 'Get up, get up!' we all yelled. He got to his feet and, bobbing under those flailing arms, he grabbed his enemy by the neck, and hung on.

The big bloke tried to shake him off, but it would have been easier to prise a limpet from a rock. Then he rose to his full height and when he did so Terry's feet left the floor – he was hanging from the bloke's neck like a pendulum!

The angry man tried to dislodge his tormentor, but Terry hung on for dear life with his face buried in his opponent's neck. Suddenly a funny look came over beanpole's face. There was a look in his eyes that denoted disbelief, then, with a frantic effort, he managed to shake off the human leech, at the same time screaming, 'I've had enough. The dirty little sod had his tongue right down my lug-hole!' And with that he scuttled out of the ring.

'What the hell did you do to him?' I asked Terrry later.

'Heh heh,' Terry chortled, 'I was trying to chew his lug!'

In the meantime, I had been given extra tuition on the rifle range – as the instructor put it, 'I think you have what it takes to be a good shot.' That pleased me not a little!

Chapter Forty-Six

There was some news waiting for me one evening early in 1927. I arrived home from work to find Mother looking rather glum, but she waited until I had eaten before telling me what was wrong.

'I've lost my job!' she wailed.

'Why?'

'Because of Bella!'

'What has she to do with you losing your job?'

'Because the man she ran away with was the husband of the manageress.'

'Well?'

'She thinks *I* had something to do with the dirty business.'

'But what about your boss, does he know about it?'

'It was he who sacked me!'

'Did he tell you why?' I asked.

'No, but he's having an affair with the manageress and he doesn't want me around in case I see too much and start talking.'

'Well you can always get another job,' I said, soothingly.

'Maybe, but not one as good.'

Had she not been near to tears I would have laughed outright, but at the same time I had to admit that she'd had a raw deal – it was indeed a right bloody carry on!

Perhaps I should explain the job Mother had. Quite unknown to Bella, she had applied for, and was given, a job as a cleaner in the cinema where Bella worked. The hours were regular and the money was decent, hence her anxiety about finding similar employment. As far as Bella was concerned, I am sure that Mother must have been aware of the intrigue, but I was certain that she took no part in the final act of their going away together.

The trouble as far as I was concerned was having to give Mother a little extra each week until she found another job, and although I honestly didn't mind – I had no wish for her to have to apply to the parish again – I began to wonder what would happen if I were to leave home for any length of time.

For instance, there was a two-week camp at Whitburn coming up, and what would prove to be more awkward was the compulsory fourteen-week training with the Navy (and I had no intention of missing that).

During the weeks that followed I noticed how withdrawn Mother had become. She would gaze pensively into the fire hour after hour, and I began to wonder whether she was missing her sister, or worrying about the future. Strangely enough, Fred wasn't unduly perturbed when I mentioned her apparent loneliness to him. 'You worry too much about her,' he said. 'I've told you before she is not an old woman, and she will soon begin making new friends. You will do well to worry about your own future.'

With only a couple of months to go, Terry and I began to look forward, with increased eagerness, to our fortnight's camp, and in the meantime we continued to make good use of the facilities on board the ship. Indeed, we were beginning to look and act like a couple of old sea-salts!

Terry especially was thoroughly enjoying himself, even though he was determined to remain an ordinary seaman. I remember him telling me – after one rather hectic training session – 'Listen chum, you can get knotted with your knots, you can box the compass until it is punch drunk, you can form fours, or fives for that matter, you can stuff your guns and rifles up the chief's arse, but I am not going to be a fuckin' sailor!'

Nevertheless, I should mention that we had both begun to view life differently since joining the reserve; we had learned the true meaning of comradeship, and I at least was convinced that the change of environment, together with being in the company of doctors, solicitors and, of course, artisans, was the primary factor in the change. It had certainly proved that my description of The Avenue as 'soul destroying' was correct, but completely inadequate. Even my pal, who had been born in the bloody place and had accepted it as the only kind of life there was, had come to realise that the world offered better things.

I had by that time qualified as a marksman on the miniature range, and was very proud to be selected for one of the two teams who competed in a local league. But I was brought down to earth when I took part in my first match, which was against the City of Newcastle rifle club – scoring just thirty out of a possible fifty. I really got the works from the captain. 'You thought you had nothing to do but pull the trigger and the bullet would find it's own way there!' What he meant was that I had become a little big-headed. Well I wasn't, not knowingly anyway, but it taught me a lesson.

Around March that year a tragic accident happened aboard the ship. A team of us were practising gun-drill when one of the lads suddenly collapsed and died.

When the captain called to see his widow, he learned that she was not too well off, so he immediately offered to provide a naval gun crew and carriage to take the place of a hearse. Everything went off perfectly on the sad day, although heaving the gun and carriage up the banks was a tough haul! Both Terry and I had volunteered to take part – we considered it a privilege.

The trouble started when we left the cemetery; it had begun to rain heavily, and when we turned into Glue House

Lane it was simply pouring. This is a particularly steep lane and we held the gun back only with great difficulty.

To ease the situation, the officer in charge brought all the men to the rear of the gun. We set off again and things were going smoothly when, without warning, the bloody gun broke loose! Of course some of the hauling ropes were still fastened to it, and the men holding them were dragged after it – Terry amongst them!

There was no way those men could halt the heavy gun, and after slithering for some distance, all but two released their hold. There was little the rest of us could do to help because we had the heavy carriage to take care of. We watched helplessly as the two men were dragged through the clarts on their bellies. Then, with a despairing yell, they too had to let go, and the gun belted away down the hill.

By the grace of God there was no traffic in the vicinity when it bounded across Scotswood Road, and had it not been for a stout wall on the other side, it would have finished it's journey in the river! But it didn't do the wall much good!

Can you guess who one of the two men was that got dragged through the clarts? Of course you can – Terry! Covered from head to toe in dirty sludge, he looked at me with disgust written all over his face, and said, 'Like I told you, stuff your fuckin' guns!'

I think it cost the ship about £100 to rebuild the damaged wall!

Chapter Forty-Seven

The weeks leading up to the camp passed all too slowly, but the week before we were due to go we had problems.

Terry and I had to inform the boss that we would be away from work for a couple of weeks and he had expressed his displeasure in no uncertain terms. In fact, he made it clear that if we went then there was the possibility of losing our jobs. Such an eventuality had never occurred to us and it put us in a flat spin.

We had to give the matter some serious thought because to lose one's job during those hard times was an act of folly. When I mentioned the problem to Fred, he quite rightly refused to offer any advice. 'It is entirely up to you,' he said.

I made up my mind to go, but Terry didn't make up his mind until the day before, when he said to me, 'Let us have a bloody good fortnight's holiday and to hell with it!'

The whole ship's company were on parade on the Saturday morning, and we stood waiting patiently for the arrival of the naval band, which was to lead us to the Central.

We waited and waited, and just as Terry asked, 'Where's the bleeding band?' three men armed with bugles got to the head of the column. When we were given the order 'quick march', those flaming buglers blared out a cacophony of such intensity that we all shuddered.

Scotswood Road wasn't too busy when we wheeled on to it, but the people who were about looked on with disbelief as those three red-faced buglers squawked out an excruciating, ear-splitting discord. It didn't help when dozens of kids decided to join in the fun and march alongside us. I could hear many of my comrades hissing out of the sides of their mouths, 'Go on, piss off,' or 'Go and get your face washed you scruffy little beggar!'

We must have been a wondrous spectacle: a trio of discordant buglers followed by two hundred pairs of feet that were hopelessly out of step. Some were marching in quick time, some in slow time, and the remainder were doing what resembled the Highland Fling!

But our troubles were as nothing compared to those of the officer leading the parade. The poor sod was only a couple of yards in front of those tortuous horns and the awful blast from them was belting on to the back of his neck! He must have reached the end of his tether when at last he turned an agonised face to them and said, 'For Christ's sake, belt up!'

Without the bugles we managed to get back into step – but the fun wasn't over yet.

Marching in a manner befitting a naval unit, we passed various groups of amused onlookers who had gathered at street corners to give us the 'once over'.

Keeping our eyes straight to the front, we approached The Avenue and, just as we reached it, there came a bellow. 'Yoo-hoo!' bawled the voice, 'Yoo-hoo, Muckian!' Terry was so startled he almost dropped his rifle. 'Sharrap!' he hissed back. But the mocking, corncrake voice had another go, 'Keep your hands over your backside, Muckian!' Poor Terry was in no position to answer but I was sure that the man responsible would pay dearly for the comments.

That humiliating march was soon forgotten when we reached the camp at Whitburn, and by the time we had drawn our bedding, listened to a lecture from the cap-

tain, then had a meal, there was only time enough to take
a stroll along the cliff top before lights out.

It was Terry's first time away from home and his reaction was typical. 'I don't know about you,' he said as we
gazed out at the North Sea, 'But I would never have
believed that one day I would be standing here dressed
in a bleeding sailor's uniform looking at a bloody ocean!'

Those of us who had considered the camp to be in the
nature of a holiday were soon disillusioned. I should stress
that the idea of coming to Whitburn camp was to make
every man proficient in the use of small arms by using the
open-air range in which the camp was situated. But there
was training in other subjects too, and the day's activities
began at the unearthly hour of 5.30 a.m. – with a strenuous
physical training period. 'It's a diabolical liberty,' said Terry.

After a couple of days, the training began in earnest,
and at last I was doing what I most wanted to do – shoot
on the open range. And it was there that I came into my
own. (Oh yes, the four-eyed old man writing this had
marvellous eyesight in those days!)

I duly qualified as a marksman, and my reward was
being selected as a member of the team which would
compete in the Northumberland championship meeting
held later that year.

How did my pal fair? Let me put it this way; we had
three instructors, each with twenty years' service in the
Royal Navy and well accustomed to dealing with awkward customers, but by the time Terry had finished with
them, one had gone prematurely grey, another developed
a nervous tic, and the third became hysterical whenever
he saw Terry with a rifle.

All too soon the final day arrived and with it the unhappy
thought of having to return to The Avenue. I think I was
more unsettled then than when I returned from Carstairs,
so the night before we were due to leave for home, Terry
and I went to Sunderland and got gloriously drunk.

Goodbye Whitburn!

Chapter Forty-Eight

We returned from Whitburn bronzed and fit on the Saturday afternoon, but we reacted in different ways. Terry was more or less glad to be back. I, however, was more unsettled than ever, but when I looked at the pasty faces of young Jim and Dora – who had never had a holiday of any kind – I was suddenly reminded of the sacrifice made by my old employer Mr Maule to help his family. I realised then that whatever ambitions I had for the future would have to be left in abeyance, at least until the two kids were older.

Mother, on the other hand, looked remarkably cheerful.

'Mother's looking very cheerful,' I said to Fred.

'She has a new friend,' he replied, rather brusquely.

'A man?'

'Yes.'

Obviously something was bothering Fred and I had to find out what it was, so I asked him.

'I know full well,' he began, 'That I haven't been able to do as much as I would have liked to, especially as far as the home is concerned, but I still have a right to know what is going on.'

'Have you had a row with her?' I asked.

He shrugged his shoulders, 'Well, sort of.' He refused to enlarge on it so I left it at that.

'What have you and Fred been arguing about?' I asked Mother.

'Who said we had?'

'He did.'

'Well, he will have to learn to mind his own business,' she snapped.

'Anything that happens in this house *is* his business,' I retorted.

She continued as though I hadn't spoken. 'I will make friends with whoever I like, and I don't care a damn whether Fred – or you for that matter – approve or not.'

I tried to point out that we had a right to be concerned, not only about her but about the two kids as well, but she wouldn't listen. Finally, I asked her if she was thinking of getting married again, but I was told not to ask any more questions. I gave it up.

Normality returned on the Monday morning. Terry had a hangover from the night before and he was in a vile mood as we made our way to Cowgate. 'If that little twat (the foreman) says a dickie to me this morning I will kick his balls off!'

Neither of us knew what to expect when we met the foreman, because he had warned us what would happen if we attended the camp. But our fears were groundless, or so it appeared.

'Hello lads,' he beamed. 'Had a good time?'

'Smashing,' we replied.

'Fine, fine,' he said with a smile.

He gently ushered us towards the door and then, still smiling, said, 'This is what I want you to do, GO AND GET YOUR FUCKIN' CARDS!'

Well, both of us had more or less expected it, but I was sure that the foreman didn't anticipate what happened next. Terry left the workshop and returned a few minutes later carrying a dustbin lid. Before I could say or do anything, he walked up to the foreman and brought the lid down with a fearful 'boing' square on the little man's bonce! 'I have wanted to do that for a long time, you little piss-pot!' shouted Terry.

Losing the job wasn't such a calamity because Terry obtained employment with a man named Ashe, and I started working for a man called Spattergood.

The remainder of that summer was quite uneventful as far as The Avenue was concerned, but along with other members of the team I practised three nights a week on the Ponteland rifle range.

When the competition opened I felt quite confident that I would give a good account of myself, but the major prizes eluded me – although I did win a bronze and a silver medal, a performance good enough to ensure my place in the team to shoot at Bisley the following year.

Terry and I were still taking advantage of the recreation facilities on the ship; we slept on board almost every weekend, and, weather permitting, we would get together a crew and row as far as Ryton Willows, have a quiet drink and then row back again. Very enjoyable it was.

It followed of course that we were spending very little time in The Avenue, but when Ma remarked, 'I'm beginning to wonder whether you live here or not,' I got very angry.

'Mother,' I said, 'I pay my board every week so what does it matter where I live or sleep? I have lived in this stinking hole for almost thirteen years and I am sick of it. I could not go to High School, you stopped me from joining the Navy, well alright, maybe I was needed at home then to keep it going, but that hardly applies now. Young Jim will soon be leaving school, you are working and you have a new friend, so why begrudge me the life I've made for myself? I'm nearly eighteen years old now and I will spend every moment I can away from this miserable place.' I think she then finally accepted the fact that I had grown up and had a mind of my own.

* * *

Positively the most exciting news that year was given to the ship's company one evening in November. The captain had addressed us, stressing the fact that we were obliged to undergo a period of training with the Royal Navy.

We were aware of that, but then he continued, 'It has been decided that the ship's company will be dispersed throughout the Home Fleet when it leaves England for the spring manoeuvres. The ship to which ratings have been posted will be on the notice board in a day or two. The exercises begin on January third.'

I rubbed my hands in gleeful anticipation of a trip abroad, but Terry wasn't too enthusiastic about leaving his job for such a long period. He was also a little sensitive about naval know-how and wasn't anxious to make a fool of himself among regular sailors. But we decided to wait and see.

He didn't attend on the evening the posters were displayed, and I anxiously scanned the list hoping to find that we would be together. Sure enough, there we were on the list under the battle cruiser *Hood*. That was really something! We were to join the world's mightiest warship!

Terry was non-committal when I told him the news. I tried to reassure him that almost every man would make a balls-up of things at first, and that the primary object was to be taught how to do things correctly. Besides, such an opportunity to see the world may never come again. Anyway, he had two months in which to make up his mind.

My *own* mind was made up – I was going!

★ ★ ★

There were only two weeks to go before we were to board the *Hood*, and I became aware that Terry's initial reluctance had returned.

'I doubt whether I shall enjoy such a long stint in the navy, so at the moment I am not sure to go,' he said. I had no intention of trying to influence him, even though he was my pal.

All preparations had been made for our departure and we were due to board the *Calliope* a few days beforehand in order to be inoculated. Terry still hadn't given any inclination as to his intentions, but his reaction to the forthcoming inoculation convinced me he would not be going.

'Balls to them and their needles,' he snapped, but I called for him on the way to the *Calliope* just in case he had changed his mind. 'I'll see you when you get back,' he said.

The medical presented no problems, but, like the rest of the men, I had a sore arse from the effects of the needle. I was about to leave the ship when, passing the medical room, I saw a familiar face looking in horror at the syringe a doctor was holding.

'What are you going to do with that bloody thing?' he asked.

'Get your trousers down,' barked the doctor.

'Eh?' gulped the startled man.

'Down with them!' bawled the doctor.

'Fuckin' hell,' groaned the dejected man, but he dropped his trousers and I barely managed to stifle a laugh as a look of agony appeared on Terry's face when he received his inoculation.

When I later asked him what had made him change his mind, he replied, 'Well, you'll need someone to look after you.'

★ ★ ★

Fred and I took a long walk the day before I left, and I told him that I had no intention of living one more day in The Avenue and that I would be doing something about it when I returned. Whatever life had in store for me, I was going to take advantage of every opportunity and use it to get away from this slum.

Fred surprised me when he told me that he planned to marry Margaret as soon as possible. The reason for the hasty marriage was the fact that his landlady had bought a house in Westmorland Road and was having it converted into bed-sits, with Fred and Margaret living in one and acting as caretakers. It was an opportunity to escape The Avenue.

Before I left he gave me a cheery smile. 'Enjoy yourself,' he said, and he meant it.

I finished my packing and wondered round to Terry's place in case he needed some assistance, but to my consternation I found him standing at his front door singing – he was plastered.

'Have you got your bag packed?' I asked.

'Bag? What bag?' he mumbled.

'Your kit bag,' I yelled at him.

He blew a raspberry. 'That to the kit bag!'

There was nothing I could do so I left him warbling away with the feeling that he would not be at the station at 7 a.m. the following morning.

My fears were realised when I knocked at his door at 6.15 the next day. 'Better make your own way lad, he doesn't look like he's getting up,' said his brother. I set off to the station alone.

Terry was still missing when the roll was called and there was no sign of him when we boarded the train, but swipe me if he didn't come tearing through the barrier with just minutes to spare. And what a state he was in!

How, I wondered, was he going to endure the rigid discipline of the Royal Navy for the three months to come? Only time would tell.

At long last I was leaving.

Goodbye The Avenue; HMS *Hood*, here we come!

Epilogue

In writing the story of my life as a boy and young man, there were times when my mental capabilities were stretched to the limit as I strove to sort out the tangled mess of nostalgia. Many times I faltered and much paper was squandered before I reluctantly came to the conclusion that it would be easier to condense the story by selecting only certain events – ones which I hope will have interested you the most.

You will have gathered that the death of my father was a devastating blow to me. He was my mentor and when I suddenly found myself bereft of his guiding hand and wisdom I became resentful, bitter, surly and, for a while at least, completely unmanageable. But the time came when I began to feel remorseful – particularly regarding Mother. I had tremendous respect for her (even though we crossed swords on many occasions) and I tried my best to help her during that very difficult period.

The joy of escaping from the filth, vermin and killer diseases of the accursed Avenue has been freely expressed in this book, but the memory of those years spent in that abominable place will be with me for the rest of my days. However, odd though it may sound, I have to admit that, if it were possible to live my life again, I would not change a thing, because were I to do so then most certainly I would forfeit the fifty years of happiness I have enjoyed since the day I met the girl I married.

Before I close the book there are two minor mysteries to clear up. The first is the long unanswered question – why did Mother move into The Avenue in the first place? For that she had to thank a certain dishonest person to whom she had given the deposit (key money) to pass on to the landlord of a house in Wharncliffe Street. It was never handed over.

How remarkably accurate Fred had been to deduce that Mother was in some kind of trouble when she had left Ashington and hurried us to Newcastle. She had been informed that the house was no longer available because the deposit had not been paid. But she was promised the tenancy of another house which was soon to become vacant, so she had moved us into The Avenue as a temporary measure. The second promise was not kept and because of it we spent almost thirteen years in hell.

The second mystery concerns the 'gargoyle' I saw standing in the passage. There is a simple answer. The wretched man had been badly burned in a fire, leaving his face scarred. His feet too had been injured and he used to shuffle up and down the stairs on his backside. Just another Avenue story!

Samuel W. Herbert